SEVEN SHADES
OF MEMORY

BY TERENCE O'DONNELL

MAGE PUBLISHERS
WASHINGTON, DC

"The Tree and the Pool" appeared previously in the Fall 1998 issue of Open Spaces

DESIGN BY MAGE PUBLISHERS
Cover/Title page photo by Mehdi Khonsari
Photo of Great Cyprus at Abarqu on pages 8-9 by M.R. Moghtader
Photo of Palace at Bagh-e Eram (Shiraz) on pages 36-37 by M. Vatankhah
Photo of Alley at Bagh-e Jannat (Shiraz) on pages 68-69 by Mehdi Khonsari
Photo of Pool at Bagh-e Mostofi (Tehran) on pages 94-95 by Mehdi Khonsari
Photo of Garden at Saadabad (Tehran) on pages 112-113 by Mehdi Khonsari
Photo of Palace Ruins at Pasargardae on pages 132-133 by Mehdi Khonsari
Author photo by Patricia Redfield

LIBRARY OF CONGRESS CATALOGING-IN-PUBLICATION DATA
O'Donnell, Terence   [1st ed]
Seven shades of memory: stories of old Iran / by Terence O'Donnell   p. cm.
Contents: The tree and the pool — The prince and the baker — The women and the ladies — The holy men
of Isfahan — The duck hunt — The stone of love — The stone of love — Mrs. Cahn
ISBN 0-934211-59-0 (paper)
1. Iran—Social life and customs Fiction   I. Title.
PS3565.D627S48 1999
813'.54—dc21
99-35117 CIP

FIRST EDITION
PRINTED AND MANUFACTURED IN THE UNITED STATES OF AMERICA
ISBN 0-934211-59-0

Mage books are available at bookstores or directly from the publisher.
To receive our latest catalog, call toll free 1-800-962-0922
or visit Mage online at www.mage.com.

For
Rosemary O'Donnell Freeman
and Robert Roy O'Donnell
with gratitude and love.

❦

for dear Thomas & Mary
with much gratitude
for their friendship.

Bernice O'D

TABLE OF CONTENTS

THE TREE AND THE POOL

THE TREE AND THE POOL

The Consul, Richard McCay, and his wife, Virginia, sat drinking martinis on the terrace of the Residence. Below lay a slope of orchard which ended, far down, at the banks of a muddy river. Figures with something red around their waists were bathing in it. Across the river stood the town: a grill of clay walls enclosing squares of green with clay cubes of buildings here and there amongst the green. Near the center, a tiled, lapis blue mosque dome rose above everything. The view held nothing else except the sky and desert.

"The problem," said the Consul, "is the tree. It's in the way." He got up and walked out to it, there at the end of the narrow lawn separating the terrace from the orchard slope. He stood, in white ducks and blue shirt, legs spread, blond head thrown back, confronting it. The tree, its trunk the girth of a millstone, rose in a slight bow to the eaves of the Residence. There, at the top, the limbs forked out, black above the Residence, into the hanging green. It was an old tree. In places it was diseased, the black bark cracked like a scab and also some of the limbs were dead. Yet it still bore fruit.

The Consul walked back to the terrace and sat down beside his wife, crooking his arm around her shoulders. She was a tall, good-looking woman with a narrow, rather sure face, dressed in a red sack dress and sandals. Sitting there, sipping her martini, she might have been back in New Haven on the terrace of the tennis club. Her husband was in his early thirties, medium height, compact, an athlete's body that had not gone slack. He had a plain, undramatic, square face with blue eyes which expressed perfect candor and much drive. They looked, their compatriots said, the ideal young American couple.

"Yes," said the Consul, "the tree's the problem. But damned if I know where else we could put the pool. There isn't enough land at the sides and the rest is hill. Even here there isn't much space; we'll have hardly any lawn left. But the tree...I don't know...it's simply in the way." He looked at his wife.

"I don't know, dear," she put her hand on his knee, "but I do know this. We'll boil in summer without the pool. Even if the Embassy, in its own sweet time, does send down the air conditioners. Who wants to stay cooped up in the house all the time? Anyway, I don't like air conditioners and I do like to swim." She threw her cigarette over the balustrade.

The Consul hitched around in his chair and, frowning, looked down at the distant figures in the river. "It's too bad we can't use that. But then it's filthy. Why they aren't all sick—but then, poor devils, they are."

"Well, dear, what to do? Could we keep the tree *and* have the pool?"

The Consul, sipping his drink, gazed at the tree. "I don't see how," he finally said. "You can't have a pool in the shade and then it's such a dirty tree, bird droppings and all the rest."

"No, we could never keep it clean and God, I'd like something clean. When I come back from the town I always feel like I should take a bath, the dust—well, in fact I do. And then, you know, really, I think I've always felt this at bottom, it gives me—the tree, I mean—the creeps, something gloomy about it," she laughed, "like the idea of God. What do I mean..." she faltered, "well, I guess I don't know exactly what I mean, exactly. I guess I

12

mean *their* idea of God. Anyway and whatever, you yourself said that the roots are probably damaging to the foundations of the Residence. Let's get rid of it, dear. I know it's big and all that and everybody talks about it but…well, I for one, am for the pool."

The Consul still gazed at the tree. "It would be a pity in a way," he finally said, "old, there so long." He looked back at his wife. "But on the other hand, it is dying. You'd really like it, wouldn't you, the pool?"

She got up, walked to the balustrade and leaned against it, her ankles crossed. "I wonder, though, what Reza and his father would say." She shook her head. "Somehow I have the feeling they won't want it touched, the old man anyway. As for Reza, I don't know. His pitch seems to be 'away with the old' no matter what. After all, he built this house for us, the only house in the place that doesn't look like some kind of fortified harem, no walls around it and real windows, no slits."

The Consul got up. "I'll see Reza tomorrow, see what he says." He took his wife's hand and crossing the terrace they went in through the French doors and mixed some more martinis.

* * *

Reza Hosseini, in an open sport shirt, tight trousers, and little Italian shoes, walked into the Consul's office at exactly the appointed time. Punctuality was one of the things he had learned while he was at school in the States. He set much store by it, as he set much store by the amulet he wore under his shirt to ward off the evil eye. He was twenty-nine and had been back two years.

"Hi Dick," he said. The Consul got up from behind his desk.

"Good morning, Reza. How are you? Please sit down." He motioned to a chair.

13

"How's it going?" Reza said. He sat down in the chair by the Consul's desk and threw one leg over the arm, a band of swarthy calf showing between the trouser cuff and the white silk ankle sock. This was another thing he had learned in the States; informality. He did not know that he sometimes misused it, that he had done so now, that the Consul was irked.

The Consul, in fact, had never much taken to Reza. So far as he could see, Reza's six years in the States had produced nothing but a degree from a poor school plus long, cheap tales about cars and girls. Nonetheless, he had one virtue, he was ready for change. And as the Consul so often said, nothing was more essential for these people than that readiness.

"Cigar, Dick?" Reza said, holding up the case. "By the way, that was a hell of a good party you put on the other night."

"No thanks, I only smoke cigars after dinner. Glad you enjoyed the party." The Consul took up a pad and pencil. "Reza, there's a project I want to discuss with you." The Consul got down to business.

It was not only the cigar he wished to refuse but the other things that went with it; the informality, the intimacy, the personal relationship as opposed to the business approach. He knew that for these people it was customary to begin everything with what for him was a prolonged and time wasting sociability. He could put up with the form so long as it had no content. But Reza, he knew, liked him, and when these people liked you it was too intimate. No, a personal relationship was only suitable in personal relationships, though he realized, uneasily, unwillingly, that for them there was no other relationship, that they did nothing without it, that they put their trust in nothing else. He knew, but he could not participate. He did not want to be Reza Hosseini's friend, but only his tenant.

The Consul lit a cigarette and waving out the match he said:

"It's a project which concerns the Residence."

"Great," said Reza. He was very proud of the Residence. It had been his idea. When the Consul had called "interesting but inconvenient" the great courtyarded native house in which he and his wife had lived at first, Reza, thinking of the American Home, had known what he meant. And so he had persuaded his father, oddly reluctant, in view of the profit to be made, to let him take their land above the river and build a Residence on it to be leased on a long term basis to the Consulate. The building of it was about the only thing he had felt good about since his return from the States. In the planning of the place, his ideal had been the cool, white colonial, a convertible parked in the drive, the kind of thing one saw in the advertisements. It had not quite turned out that way, but it didn't matter. There it was on the hill for all to see, something new he had made, no walls around it, picture windows, and, as he bragged to his uncomprehending friends, there were three toilets.

"A project for the Residence?" Reza repeated. "I'm all ears."

The Consul drew a rectangle on the pad. "A pool," he said. "A swimming pool. We think, Virginia and I, that it would make all the difference. And it's certainly something the consuls after me would appreciate. We—"

"What a neat idea!" Reza interrupted.

"Yes," the Consul said, "as I was saying, we—that is the Consulate—would be prepared to pay half the cost, an arrangement which I should think you and your father would be agreeable to. There is, however, one problem—"

"Dick, it's colossal, a wonderful idea." Reza settled back in the chair and cocked one leg over the other. He waved the cigar. "You'll have a little bar, I suppose, and..." he laid his head back, staring at the ceiling, "pool parties." He thought of the women. It was one of the things he missed—not the sex itself. He had his mistress and his trips to the capital. It was the preliminaries which were missing. He thought again, as he often did, of the pastel jersey rump crowning a barstool, the dancing, the fast, powerful drive with the top down, the snug motel. And the motel reminded him of a night when he and a group of people had come out of their units to swim, drunk, in the motel pool. "Dick, I got to tell you." He was up, standing by the desk, leaning over the Consul. "A pool party one night at a motel, the lights out, Christ." He saw the Consul frown. "Of course, I know you wouldn't be having that kind of thing at the Residence." He looked away. "It's just that it reminded me." Embarrassed, he laughed. Then he slowly went back to his chair and sat down. The cigar gone out, he turned it between his fingers. "Anyway, it's a nice idea. It'll be nice for you and Virginia."

"The pool isn't built yet, Reza. What I wanted to tell you is that there is a problem. I don't know, perhaps we can't build it at all." The Consul began drawing on the pad again. "The only level place large enough is the lawn. But the tree is in the way." He threw down the pencil. "If we want the pool, the tree will have to go. That's what I wanted to ask you about."

"The tree?" said Reza, as though he didn't understand. "Oh, the big tree. Yes. It's in the way? You couldn't leave it? Isn't it almost at the end of the lawn anyway?"

"It's the branches, Reza. There'd be no sun. Also, the roots would break through the walls of the pool in time. No, I'm afraid it's the tree or the pool."

Reza didn't answer. His father, he knew, would object. It was like everything else. When he came back there had been so many things he had wanted to change. In the beginning he had met with indifference. Then, pushing a little harder, downright opposition. It had happened at home with his

16

family, at the agricultural office with his boss. They held on to whatever was old, whether it was a thing or a way of doing something. The tree would be the same. "I'll try," he said at last, not looking at the Consul, the breeze and boldness gone out of him. "But my father is old-fashioned, you know. The tree—it's been there a long time. They're funny about trees." He laughed, "About a lot of things. He'll probably say that there's the river for swimming."

"Oh, the river is out of the question," said the Consul, pushing the pad aside. "You know yourself that it's dirty. In fact, by rights, people should be prevented from bathing there." He stopped. An idea had come to him, his blue eyes staring into it. "Reza!" He got up from the desk and came out into the room, standing, his hands on the back of his hips. "You gave me an idea. You mentioned pool parties. Why not! Though not exactly," he laughed, "the kind you have in mind. Listen Reza." He sat down on a corner of the desk. "There's no real swimming pool in the town. Right? I know, there're the little pools in every courtyard to wash in before you pray, I know, but if you'll forgive me, you wash everything else in them as well. Anyway, they're not big enough to swim in, for real exercise, laps. So what about this. We build the pool, a filter system and the works and then we'll invite special groups, the health department people, the Governor, the rest, and perhaps they'll get the idea. I mean—well, I mean simply that it might activate them to build a public pool." The Consul stood up. "What do you think? I might even be able to get one of our agencies interested in it. Think of the step toward sanitation. And also—and you know what I think about this—it would give the people, especially the young people, something to do! Swimming classes, first aid, competitions, that kind of thing. What do you think?"

17

"I think you're right," said Reza. "Something to do." It was this which had driven him half mad his first year back; no bars, no clubs, no roads for his sports car. Nothing but the evening promenades, the Friday picnics, the long hours lolling in a teahouse, hunting sometimes in the mountains. "It's a great idea, Dick, a—a public service." And as he said it, he thought again of the women. Perhaps there would be secretaries down from the Embassy. Then he remembered the tree and his father. "The problem is the old man."

"And problems are to be overcome," said the Consul. He immediately realized how pompous it sounded. "I'm sorry, Reza. But still it's up to you. Talk to your father, see what you can do." He put the pad away. "I'll hear from you." He wanted to end the meeting.

"Right," said Reza. "I'll sure do what I can." He sprawled out in the chair. "So how's Virginia? What have you been up to anyway?"

"Oh, not much." The Consul stood up. "Forgive me, Reza. I've this other appointment." He realized how abrupt it must sound. Coming out from around the desk, he took Reza's hand. "Drop by tomorrow for a drink."

"Great," said Reza, his face brightening. "And the pool, leave it to me, Dick. I'll get it done, one way or the other. You'll see."

"That's the spirit, Reza, and thank you for coming in," the Consul said as he withdrew his hand from the pressure of Reza's.

* * *

The following day Reza telephoned to say that his father would not give permission to remove the tree. It was with effort that the Consul stifled his anger. He thought of Virginia and her disappointment. He thought too of the collapse of his plan to provide the town with the example of the pool. Couldn't Reza try his father again? No, it was useless. "Perhaps you give up too easily," the Consul had said. He immediately regretted the words. He regretted them even more, a few weeks later, when the leaves of the tree turned black.

It was Virginia, fastening a bird feeder to the sill of an upstairs window, who first noticed it. "Dick," she called to the Consul, who was sitting below on the terrace. "The leaves have gone all funny. Can you see it from down there?"

"What?" he said, walking out on to the lawn and peering up. "No, what do you mean?" And then he went upstairs to stand by his wife. The leaves at the end of some of the upper branches were shriveled, ashen, as though they had been seared by fire. "Some sort of pest, I imagine," the Consul said.

A few days later it happened. The tree had always been an enormous, natural aviary of birds. Taking their tea on the terrace, the Consul and his wife were suddenly aware that the tree was silent and looking up they saw that all the birds had left. In the week that followed the tree began to drop its blackened leaves, like factory smuts across the grass, acrid, souring the air.

At first the Consul had been puzzled, then suspicious. In the old days in the country, when you wanted to get rid of a man you poisoned him. Why not the same for a tree. The Consul sent a little earth from the base of the tree to a laboratory in the capital. The report which came back stated that the earth contained high amounts of lye.

Instead of telephoning, the Consul decided to go to Reza's office. He crossed the courtyard of the Department of Agriculture to the outside stairway leading up to Reza's office. There was a pool in the courtyard, scummy with unchanged water, a few rickety benches, and beyond the pool an arbor, leaning, on the point of collapse. Here, beneath the arbor, the usual peasants squatted, waiting to air their complaints. They watched the Consul crossing the courtyard, fresh in seersucker and a blue, button-down shirt. When he drew near, they stood up, big men in indigo smocks and full black trousers. As he passed, they bowed and touched their hearts. The Consul inclined his head and said good morning.

Before the Consul reached the top of the staircase, Reza, hearing steps, was on the landing. "Dick!" he cried. Surprised, and very pleased, he threw out his arms in welcome. Then he clattered down the steps and took the Consul's hand, holding it, leading the Consul up the steps. He was overwhelmed with pleasure. "I'm so glad," he kept repeating. It was the first time the Consul had called on him. He wanted to embrace and kiss him as he would have done with one of his friends. Instead he held on to the hand, though he felt its pull, until they were in the office. Then he took the chair which stood in front of his desk, carried it around, and put it next to his own. He dusted it off with his sleeve and patting the seat said, "Come, Dick, sit down." The Consul remained standing.

"I've only a minute," the Consul said, looking around the room. It was a shoebox set on end, a door on one side with a dirty transom, a window opposite. Between these stood Reza's desk, ponderous, its veneer buckling. There was an old-fashioned inkstand of curlicue iron, an empty in-and-out box, and a china lady whose loins formed an ash-tray. Above on the wall hung an oleograph of the Prophet, below Reza's college pennant.

The Consul walked to the window and leaned against the jam. "I've come about the tree," he said. Reza, tipped far back in the swivel chair, his legs crossed, fingered his tie and smiled.

"The tree—?" Reza repeated. "Oh, the big tree. Why? What about it?" He was still smiling. The Consul watched him. He was sure—almost—that it was Reza who had killed the tree. He hoped not, remembering his own last words to Reza on the subject of the tree. But he hadn't had in mind this way—their way—of doing things. Looking hard at Reza, hoping to disconcert him and so find out the truth he said: "It's dead."

Reza inclined his head slightly, looking steadily back. "Really." Then he came slowly forward in the chair and put his elbows on the desk. "I wonder... Yes, I bet that's it. I'd even forgotten myself. At that garden party of yours someone was saying—who was it—that the ice cream man emptied out his brine tub down there at the end of the lawn. I should have told you, I..."

"Could a tub of brine kill a tree that size?"

Reza looked at him for a moment before turning away. He opened a drawer and took out a pack of American cigarettes. Then he swung back, grinning. "I think we can say so, Dick."

The Consul straightened suddenly and stepped away from the window. He wanted to walk out of the room, out of the complicity. He had wanted the tree gone but not with a lie and worse, this cock-and-bull story of a brine tub no more than a front for one of Reza's people creeping in at night and soaking the ground with lye. "It's a very unfortunate business," he finally said, not looking at Reza, frowning, his mouth tight.

"What? What's unfortunate?" Reza asked, rising a little from his chair. "I thought you wanted the pool. Now we can have it. No sweat. I don't understand, Dick."

"No matter," the Consul replied. "I take full responsibility. I mean, I'll pay whatever the tree was worth." And then he remembered that it was Reza's father for whom the tree had value and so the father should set the price. Going to the father would be distasteful but it was the proper thing to do. "Yes, I'll pay," he went on, "but I'll make the arrangements with your father."

"My father! Why?"

"I prefer it that way."

Reza shrugged. "Anyway you want. But it might not be a bad idea if you mentioned the ice cream man emptying the tub."

The Consul walked to the door. He reached for the handle and then turned back. "No, I won't mention the brine tub."

"What about the pool, then" Will you mention that?"

"The pool," the Consul repeated. "I don't know." He went out the door.

"Dick," Reza called, following him. "Dick," he called again when he reached the landing. The Consul, halfway down the steps, turned and looked back at him. "I'm sorry Dick. Really I'm sorry. I thought it was what you wanted." The Consul went down the steps.

*　*　*

The black, consular Cadillac, with its little fender flags, slowly nosed into the square of the old town, then stopped before a confusion of carts, animals, and men. The driver roared his motor and honked his horn and the car went slowly on, rocking down into the deep ruts, raising dust, stopping sometimes for a cart to turn out of the way. The Consul, very straight, sat in the back, looking out. These things—the crowds, the confusion, the noise, the feeling that he was at the heart of the real city—made him wonder about the time he spent with the officials in the new town. He knew that in all but the poorest houses of the city there was a special room set aside for visitors, rooms, it seemed to him, in which order had been nailed down and cleanliness, like a fixative, sprayed on, gaunt rooms which, however many heaters brought in, stayed cold. He knew too that behind these rooms the true life of the

22

house went on; noisy, casual, crowded. Here, now, in the square, he felt that he had passed from the room for the visitors into the place where the people lived.

The big car lurched on across the square, gained the street on the other side, and then, after a short distance, stopped before the entrance to a narrow lane. The Consul got out, buttoned his coat, and started down the lane, the driver walking behind him.

High blank walls rose on either side of him, of clay, like the lane itself. It seemed to the Consul as if he were in some desert village rather than at the very center of the city. Then they passed the first of the great doors, gates, really, of paneled wood, studded, and with knockers of brass shaped like a hand. They were all closed except one, slightly ajar. The Consul glanced in, his vision of the courtyard blocked by a screen wall of open brickwork. It annoyed him that he could still be irked by these excluding walls, just as it annoyed him that he could not accept the deference which made his driver walk behind him rather than abreast. He knew the reason for the deference and the walls, for all the other differences, but knowing the reasons did not seem to be enough. Perhaps nothing was enough. For a moment he gave in, and looking down at the dust which filmed his shoes, he wondered why the hell the lazy bastards didn't pave the lane.

They stopped at a gate no different from the others and the driver banged the knocker. They heard the thudding of running steps. The gate scraped open and a barefoot servant stepped back to let them enter. They were in a small, domed vestibule, white-washed, the clay brick floor freshly wetted. There was a bench against the opposite wall and above, in a niche, a big green jar of laurel. From somewhere the Consul heard bird song.

Following the servant, the Consul went through an arch to the right and down three steps into the garden. It was a small orchard, really, rather than a garden, but laid out with beds and walks—one of those many enclosures of green which one could see from the Residence. It stretched some distance between white walls to a long, low house. At the end where the Consul stood, glass sloped down from the whole length of the lane wall to form a greenhouse, brilliant with geraniums and bougainvillaea. The Consul knew, had remembered when walking in the dry gully of the lane, that behind the walls there were usually courts or gardens tropical with vegetation. Yet the contrast always surprised and puzzled him.

He walked on slowly in the sun, down the center path. Now he saw from where the bird song came. To his left a line of blind arches were set into the garden wall and from the center of each hung a bell-shaped bamboo cage of birds. He went on, feeling suddenly rested, wishing he had no business there but could simply stroll instead and when he reached the pool where the garden's four paths met he paused at a bench which stood in the shadow of a heavy mulberry. But he went on— and then stopped, sensing that his driver was not behind him. He looked back and saw the man stooping to float an open rose on the black surface of the water, then straightening up and gazing down at it. The Consul walked on, out into the sun, and toward the house.

A curtain of green and white striped canvas hung across almost the whole facade. As they approached, it parted at the center and an old man in a black skull cap and a loose black coat came out. His eyes down, he walked slowly up the path, while the Consul hurried forward. The Consul introduced himself. The old man bowed. Then they walked together toward the house, the Consul stooping a little toward the old man. "I hope, Haji

Abbas, that I have not come at an inconvenient time," he said.

The old man gestured with his hand. "You bring honor to this garden," he said, perfunctorily, not looking at the Consul, walking on. When they reached the house, two servants drew back the part in the canvas and they stepped up on to the long, darkened veranda. In front of him the Consul saw a French door open to a room and beyond, across the room, another French door open to a second courtyard. Haji Abbas, at the doorsill, stepped out of his little, white twill slippers. The Consul stooped too, and undoing the laces, pulled off the big brogues. He pushed them to one side with his foot. Then he stooped again and placed the shoes neatly, side by side before the sill.

They walked into the room. Haji Abbas motioned toward one end and said: "Please be seated." The Consul looked and saw a blanket laid next to the wall, surrounded on three sides by bolsters. For a moment he hesitated, and then walked over and sat down, cross-legged on the floor. It was the first time he had been in a house in which a chair had not been brought out for the foreign guest. Was this now, he wondered, a discourtesy or simply unself-consciousness before the Westerner?

Across from him, Haji Abbas sat, hands in his lap, saying nothing. He was a little man with a pale, pointed face and large cold eyes. In the fine bones of the face and fingers, in some blend of aloofness and repose he was mandarin—almost. For the Consul sensed that there was temper in him and some kind of ungenerous quickness, that he was not detached. It seemed impossible that this could be the father of the sleek and easy Reza.

"You will take some refreshments?" Haji Abbas asked, closing his eyes, as if weary or disinclined toward the formulas of hospitality. "Akbar," he softly called, his eyes still closed. A servant entered from the courtyard carrying two silver trays. One held lime-water and ice in big glasses set in silver holders, the other a plate of petal-thin pastries convoluted in the forms of flowers.

The Consul took a lime-water and began. "I have come about the tree."

"Shall we take our refreshments first?" Haji Abbas replied. So without speaking they drank the lime-water and the Consul looked around the room. It was empty except for a carpet, the blanket, and the bolsters. The carpet, an Isfahan, had a cream ground patterned with arabesques and flowers in red, gentian blue, buff, and green. The bare walls were the cream of the carpet's ground and divided into panels framed with plaster moldings. On the ceiling the kinds of designs which patterned the carpet were reproduced in painted plaster relief, while on the small, blunted cusps formed by the converging whorls of the plaster there were frescoed miniatures—a garden, a bridge, lovers, mustachioed doe-eyed warriors. The Consul had never seen such a room before and he was confused by its contradictions; it was so empty and so full, so lavish and so simple. He was impressed by the carpet and the ceiling but on the whole he thought he preferred the bland, straightforward walls.

The old man put down his glass with a clatter. "So you are here about the tree. I understand that it is dead."

"Yes, I am sorry to say." It was a relief to be down to business. He would express his regrets, pay whatever was required, and finish the matter. "As you know, we wanted to build a swimming pool at the Residence. The tree was in the way. Therefore, I asked your son if it might be removed—with proper compensation, of course. Apparently you were unwilling."

"Yes, I was unwilling."

"I see," the Consul said slowly, careful now, for there had been rancor in the old man's voice. The Consul leaned forward. "I will be frank with you. We wanted the tree gone.

When you refused we were disappointed. But, believe me, this—this accident, whatever happened, was not my doing. Again, yes, I wanted the tree gone but I was quite ready to respect your wishes in the matter and furthermore, and this is what is important, I did." The Consul leaned back, an earnest, satisfied expression on his face.

"And now you will build the pool?" the old man asked.

"Why, yes, I guess so, if you are agreeable, why? After all, the tree is gone, or rather will be. That is one of the matters I wanted to discuss with you today. With your permission I'll have it cut down and taken away."

Haji Abbas began to slowly rock back and forth. "I see," he said, "so you will have your pool," and he smiled crookedly, "you will have your way."

"Do you think it need be put in those terms? I have told you that however much I may have wanted the pool, I sincerely regret the way in which this has come about. But it has come about and as we say in English, the past is past. Apparently the tree meant much to you and I—"

"Do you have any idea why?"

The Consul started to reply, then stopped. After a moment he said:

"No, no I really don't know why. It was big...?"

"I wonder, should I tell you." The old man hunched his shoulders and then let them fall with a sigh. "And anyway, you are probably in a hurry."

"No," said the Consul, who was.

"Really?" replied the old man. "That surprises me." And he gave the Consul his bitter little smile. "Come, let us go to the garden. We often do this when we talk—stroll together. I am told you do everything from desks?"

"No," said the Consul, irritated by the comment, thinking of the business lunches and the golf course.

So they went into the garden and began to walk the path which bordered the arched wall.

"Here we are," Haji Abbas said. "And if you find me tiresome," he laughed, "you may listen to the birds." He paused at one of the cages, his head cocked, and began to snap his fingers near the bars. Then he turned back. "To begin, I think I should tell you something about the Residence. I mean about the place itself before we built the house. You are interested in the history of things?"

"Of course, when it has some bearing on the present."

"Doesn't it always?"

"Yes, sometimes too much," the Consul said. The little, pointed face turned toward him.

"Ah, I see," the old man said at last. "Well, nonetheless, to go on. One day when I was a boy—fourteen or fifteen—my father took me to the place where the Residence now stands. It wasn't my first time there, of course—the family used it sometimes for picnics. But this time we went alone, the two of us, and even now I can remember how I felt that something special was to happen. I remember too what a fine day it was, spring, all the blossoms and the wind, and I feeling that restlessness of boys, not wanting to be with my father and that constraint. And then my father did a most extraordinary thing, as if he knew my feelings—and of course he did. He reached across—we were taking our lunch on a carpet under the tree—and put into my hand the key of the place, the key to the gate. I can remember now how he pressed my fingers around it and told me that from now on I was to consider the garden as my own...as a private place to go."

Haji Abbas, who had been walking with head down, stopped and looked up at the Consul. "I hope you will not find this subject indelicate, your Excellency. You must forgive me."

"Not at all; it's very interesting. Please go on."

"You see, our custom—more so in that time than now—was to marry our boys as soon as they, well, as soon as they were men. If for some reason that was not practical, then it was common to have a good-looking maidservant in the house. My father, I knew, disapproved of this. Even more he disapproved of the brothels, not because of the reason for going to them or because of the women themselves but because he thought brothels ugly and unseemly for such purposes. Love, as he told me that day in the garden, should be made in a beautiful place." The old man stopped and pointed to a bench. "Shall we sit for a moment? There is a view here of the mosque."

The Consul looked and saw the glistening lapis dome beyond the walls and rooftops. It looked so different from the Residence, pale and insubstantial, whereas here, close by, it was for him as it had never been before, entirely real.

"So," the Consul said at last, turning to the old man, "your father gave you the garden." And as he said it he thought of his own boyhood adventures in the motels off the interstates.

"Yes," said the old man. He laughed. "And I used it for the purpose given. I don't think I ever missed, at least in the temperate months, a full moon night. I would find some girl, disguise her as a boy—so as not to cause scandal, you see—and take her up there on the bar of my bike. Sometimes too I would go with friends and we would carry on, gamble, drink, bang a drum, one of us would dance. It must be the same in your country. Boys like to have someplace to go off to and be wild. In any event, we did. Sometimes too we would share a girl and stay on till dawn and then go back to town and to the baths to cleanse ourselves and afterwards be at the bazaar fresh and ready for the day's work." He turned to the Consul. "Shall we walk again?"

They went down the path, Haji Abbas bent forward, his hands, behind his back, strung with black prayer beads. Against the silence of the garden the Consul listened to the clicking beads and thought of then and now, of the boy in the other garden banging a drum, of the old man now walking the path in the shadow of the mosque dome. To the Consul, youth and age have always seemed like broken parts. Here, with the old man, he sensed a life which had moved like the line of the dome, slowly growing into amplitude, now gently bending inwards toward completion. Here it seemed the parts were whole.

"I didn't know," the Consul said at last, "that the place was special for you. I thought it was just a property you had."

"No," Haji Abbas replied. "And that is why when Reza approached me with the plan for building the Residence I hesitated. It was not only memories. I thought Reza would like the place, would use it as I had done. But Reza..." he stopped, his eyes moving around the garden as if searching for something. "Reza has become different from us. He seems to prefer...hotel rooms." The old man looked at the Consul, his eyes wide, uncomprehending, hurt. "I find it very strange," he said.

"I see," the Consul said, not knowing exactly what he meant by his own words, whether it was the hotel room which he understood or that he shared the old man's wonder at Reza's preference.

"At any rate," Haji Abbas went on, "there was the place no longer used, Reza indifferent to it, and after all money to be made—good money—by leasing it to you. So I agreed. But on one point," he looked up, frowning at the Consul, "I was adamant; the tree was not to be touched. Even then, Reza wanted to get rid of it, something about its crowding the house. 'No,' I told him, 'the tree must stay.'"

He stopped, turned away from the Consul, and looked out

over the garden, his hands stroking the leaves of a lilac which grew by the path. "Everything," he went on quietly, "has its heart; a body, a house, a garden. And that tree was the heart of the garden. I mean the love that was made under it. I mean the branch which showed us the direction of Mecca when we prayed. I mean its fruit, served at my wedding feast. I think of the spring when it put out more blossoms than the sky has stars and crowned the garden like a sign from God." His hand, trembling among the lilacs, suddenly ripped away a leaf. "So," he said, turning back to the Consul. The leaf fell to the ground. He stopped, peering down at it, and then straightening, he slowly mashed it into the gravel with his foot.

The Consul looked away, wondering if this wasn't simply an old man's sentimentalism soured by peevishness. There was nothing in his own past, no experience, no place, which had left more than a faint imprint. One went on to something new. What one wanted was now or ahead, not behind. "The pool," he said, gently touching the old man's shoulder. "Don't you think the pool will make up for it? After all, every generation has its playthings and they change." He laughed. "When Reza is an old man he'll probably think about the pool as you have talked about the tree. Moreover—and I am sure Reza told you about this—we thought the pool would be such a good example for the town. The river, the river is filthy, Haji Abbas. You must know that. And these small pools in every courtyard, and you must forgive me, Haji Abbas, but they aren't exactly clean either, fed as they are from the river water and, well, for other reasons as well. The swimming pool, however, would have a special mechanism to clean the water. A real place to swim, and people here have so little recreation."

"Yes, the pool," Haji Abbas said, grimly, as someone who has been robbed might say the word "thief." "Reza told me all about it. It was to be," he laughed, "so clean, as you say. And a cement terrace around it with chairs and, I believe, some kind of umbrella to give shade in place of the tree. It was all to be such an improvement. What good did it do to remind Reza of the time when my brother, returning from pilgrimage to Mecca, was honored there in the garden? We laid out carpets, dozens of them, in a solid circle around the tree. Can you imagine the sight! Cement!" he said abruptly. "Yes, no wonder you use chairs. I could never understand your custom; they hold one so, separating one from other people, unnatural contrivances it seems to me. But with cement—yes, I see. One would want a chair."

"Our customs are different," the Consul said.

"Of course they are. And ours, your Excellency, are different from yours—and you are here."

"I haven't forgotten that."

"I wonder. I think you have. Or if you haven't forgotten, then there are certain of our customs and beliefs which you have simply disregarded. Do you permit me to explain?"

"As you wish."

"You have told me that our river and our pools are filthy. Yet you know, don't you, that if Reza bathed in your pool he would become, in our religious view, unclean."

The Consul flushed. He knew that according to the letter of the religious law he was unclean since as a non-Moslem he did not perform the rites of ablution laid down by Islam. And how it angered him when he thought of the filth of the river, the filth of the streets, the flies, the offal.

"However," Haji Abbas continued, "I am sure you understand, for Reza tells me that in your country there are people whom you consider unclean. We find it odd though that they are your fellow countrymen as well as your co-religionists!"

The Consul wondered what he meant. Then he understood. "Oh, you mean our blacks, segregation and so forth. Well, that's a special problem, of course, a long, complicated history behind it and, of course, we've done a great deal to remedy the situation."

"Ah I see. Then that is what you meant when you said that the past sometimes has too much bearing on the present. I had thought you meant us... Well, I suppose there isn't too much more to say. You may take away the tree of course. After all it's dead. Yes, and you will pay for it."

"I am sorry there is this bitterness," the Consul said. "I don't know what else to say; only that I regret it. I hope that you believe me."

The old man turned and looked at him and for the first time it seemed to the Consul that the hostility had left his eyes.

"Yes," he said, "I believe you. But what is your regret if it is not the beginning of something else. Someone once told me a saying of your people, from one of your writers perhaps: that East is East and West is West and that they will never meet. That, of course, is not true, or at any rate true no longer; even I know that. But what is happening now, your Excellency, is a collision, not a meeting, and I believe that we are being injured by the impact. I know there is much in our old way which is diseased, dead, but we must bend into change, into newness, not be fractured...for then, you see, there will be no connection. Look at Reza, my poor boy. Is that a meeting...poor mangled boy?"

The Consul looked at his watch. "When will you let me know about the tree, its price?"

"Its price," the old man repeated. "Oh, later. I shall send you a bill."

"Then, if you will forgive me, I must go." The Consul put

out his hand. Haji Abbas touched the Consul's fingertips and bowed. Without speaking they walked toward the gate. When they reached the pool, Haji Abbas stooped and took the rose which still floated on its surface and gave it to the Consul.

* * *

At the Consulate the Consul gave orders for the tree to be removed immediately and then set to work on some reports. At 6:30 he sent a message to his wife that he still had work to do and would take his supper at the Consulate. It was late by the time he returned to the Residence to sleep.

He woke at dawn, and unable to go back to sleep and thinking that what he needed was air, he got up and went to the window. His face close to the window screen, he was suddenly assailed by its smell, a whiff of something acid. At the same time he heard the soft fluttering of a moth on the other side, beating against the wire. A muscle knotted in his throat. He swallowed and shook his head, feeling slightly faint and then he looked down to the place where the tree had been. He saw simply its absence, emptiness. Staring down at the emptiness in the growing light, the question, slowly, painfully, formed in his mind, and he began to wonder with what the tree, with what the pool, might be replaced.

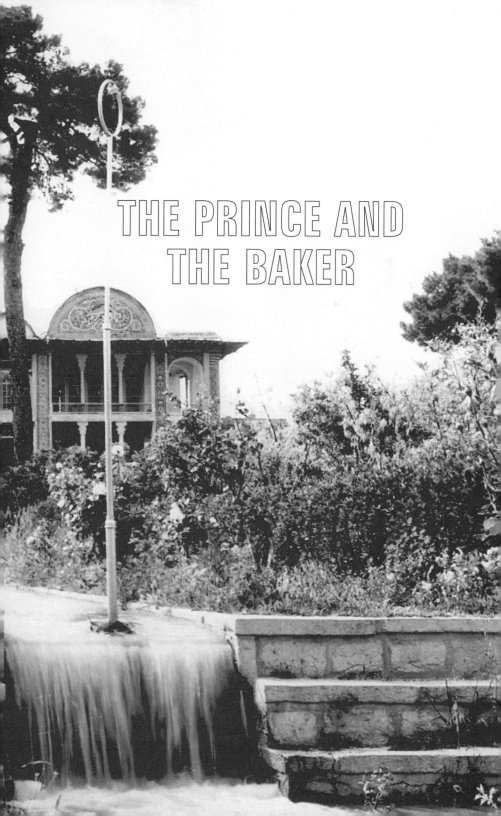

THE PRINCE AND
THE BAKER

THE PRINCE AND THE BAKER

It has been said that on occasion life has more imagination than we do. Thus it was that at the end of a long life Prince Mansour Doleh was taken by surprise.

The Prince lived in an old and rambling house in the depths of the city. The house stood at the end of a narrow lane, its great outside gates set into a covered masonry structure hung with tiled stalactites. From the gates a passage through roses and almond trees led to the house itself. Inside an entrance hall-cum-gallery stretched some sixty feet along the front of the house. Fourteen crystal chandeliers sparkled down the gallery's length, flinging shimmers of opalescent light against the gallery walls, the walls themselves hung with banners and flags, sabers, pieces of armor, and antique tapestries. At the end of the gallery stood the Prince's most prized possession, a music box, an enormous contraption which, in addition to the spiked cylinder contained miniature bells, tambourines, and drums which clanged and thumped as the machine pinged out its old Viennese waltzes.

The gallery gave off on to several salons. Like the gallery, these were hung with banners and flags as well as some price-less seventeenth century Persian carpets. On every table stood gilded gifts from half the crowned heads of Europe. There were also a number of photos, all of the Prince as a young man excepting one in which as a child he was being dandled on the ample haunch of the Agha Khan. Others showed him as a page at the court of George V, sitting with his father and Franz Joseph in a garden at Schönbrunn, another with his father and Tzar Nicholas II on a yacht in the Baltic, and an especially dashing photo of himself dancing with the Duchess of Luxembourg in some grand ballroom on the Riviera. The salons were rarely used now and despite their opulence were dusty and damp, some of the walls even water-stained.

On those rare occasions when the Prince did receive a visitor a certain protocol was observed. At the first squeak of the outside gates, old Fatemeh, the Prince's maid and majordomo, would set the music box going. After the guest had entered and been led down the gallery to see the workings of the marvelous machine, the Prince himself would descend the stairway at the opposite end of the gallery and call out a ringing "hallo"—like the first appearance of the tenor on a light opera stage. After pausing for a moment at the foot of the stairs, he would then march down the gallery to receive his guest, his gait measured to the beat of the music box tune.

On these occasions the Prince looked like an ex-guardsman: very tall, very straight, his thick mane of hair and grand mustache even blacker than in his youth, his cheeks rosy (only a touch of rouge), his eyes flashing between the kohl-stained lids. On these occasions he would, of course, get out of his old, frogged dressing gown and into one of the London tailored, pin-striped suits, a gardenia in the buttonhole, a handkerchief of the finest lawn tucked into his sleeve. The Prince would greet his guest in French or German or English or Persian, whichever was required, and then take the guest by the arm and turn him into one of the more presentable salons with the same grace as, in the past, he would have turned his partner in a waltz.

Over tea in the Sevres cups, the Prince would captivate his guest with a combination of great charm and exquisite manners, so much so that on leaving the visitor would reflect that in both appearance and demeanor Prince Mansour Doleh was indeed a prince, every inch. He would also marvel at so much vitality in one so old.

But after the guest had in fact left, the curtain would fall and the Prince would slump in his chair, exhausted by his performance, the touch of rouge now brilliant against the ashen cheeks. Old Fatemeh knew to come. She would pull him out of the chair, help him up the stairs to his sitting room and bedroom—the two rooms in which he lived—lay him out on his bed, bring him a glass of brandy, and then remove his shoes and massage his feet until he fell asleep. Sometimes she would stand there looking down at him, remembering, this big, heavy, country woman, her coarse hands flashing with jewels, her ankles, above the big, bare feet, circled by gem-encrusted, gold anklets. Yes, remembering, for in her youth she had been the Prince's favorite mistress and because, it was said, she then had the most beautiful eyebrows in the kingdom.

Fatemeh was in fact about the same age as the Prince, both in their middle nineties. She took her age and its ailments with good peasant sense and anyway hadn't the Prophet written that old age is a sickness for which there is no cure? In general, Fatemeh was grateful for her long life with its mixture of tears and laughter—and for the jewels, too, just in case, for you never knew… When, in the afternoon, she sat on her scrap of carpet by the courtyard pool, her hands folded in her lap, she was at peace.

The Prince was not. Looking back he saw a life of great privilege, many pleasures, a few honors. But now as he more and more heard the creaking wings of the angel of death, there were less happy memories, too, and it was these and the remorse they engendered which stooped his shoulders far more than age.

It was for this reason that the Prince seldom ventured out anymore into the city in his old, plum-colored Rolls Royce. By way of explanation for what follows it should be noted that the Prince's fellow citizens were famous in Persia for their cutting wit, a wit which now in old age cut the Prince deeply indeed. When, for example, passing in the old plum-colored limousine, some rapscallion or other would call out the scurrilous epithet which the people had bestowed upon him and which went as follows: "You murdered your mother, you sold your country, and you fuck your sister."

Truth in Persia is like a lump of clay. Shaped by the potter's hand, it may result in a bowl of exquisite beauty or an object of inexpressible ugliness—depending. In the case of the Prince, there may have been some truth in the scurrilous epithet but how much it is difficult to say. Even the Prince was not entirely certain, so many years having passed since the alleged transgressions. However, to the best of his failing memory the circumstances giving rise to the charges were the following.

Once, when the Prince was no more than a boy, his mother fell out with the Prince's father. In the altercation which followed, she fled to a mosque, a place of sanctuary in Persia. It was said that the boy was sent to the mosque by his father to bring the woman out, and should she refuse, he was to kill her. The Prince's recollection was that his mother refused to leave, and that on doing so, a stranger appeared and shot her. It was true that the boy was so positioned that if he had wished he could have knocked the weapon from the assailant's hand. But he did not do so, fearing his father's famous wrath.

As for the charge that he had sold his country, it was true that he had engaged with foreigners in various negotiations concerning the Persian oil fields. It was true as well that as the result of those negotiations he had himself benefited handsomely. On the other hand, in his judgement his country had benefited too—though there were those who might have disputed that claim.

The third charge was even more murky. One winter's day, again in youth, the Prince and his sister had on impulse gone off to the family hunting lodge in the mountains. The servants, not informed of their coming, had not prepared the charcoal for the braziers—a rather lengthy procedure—and the wood for the great fireplace was found to be too wet to burn. Chilled, the Prince and his sister climbed into bed to cuddle and so warm themselves. Had something happened? The Prince could not quite remember. Whatever the truth, the spying servants believed something had, and thus was the story spread.

These, then, were the memories which darkened the Prince's days, for he knew— despite the readiness of the people to exaggerate for the sake of wit and despite his own failing memory—knew nonetheless that there was some truth in the allegations and that it was an ugly truth. Try as he might, he could not expunge from his mind this sense of a soiled life. So it was, when looking down from his sitting room at old Fatemeh, there in the courtyard on her scrap of carpet, her hands folded in her lap, that he so envied her peace. In his sorrow, he had no intimation, of course, of the surprise that lay in store for him.

II: THE BAKER

The Prince and the baker had long been neighbors. That a Prince and a simple baker could be neighbors may seem strange to a Westerner. Traditionally, however—and still to some extent—the rich and the poor, the lofty and low, all lived together in the one neighborhood or quarter. Indeed from the Prince's great gates it was only a few steps down the lane to the baker's house with its little door. This door, by the way, was so low that to enter one was obliged to stoop; *dar bandegi*, the baker called it, the door of humility.

As mentioned above, the Prince and the baker had long known each other. For years they had passed in the lane, the Prince inclining his head, the little baker bowing low, his hand across his heart, both mumbling Koranic blessings to each other. Also, on those occasions when the Prince held a *nazr*— a thanksgiving to God for some favor bestowed and which took the form of a banquet to which all members of the quarter were invited, especially the poor—the baker was always among the guests. Also in the mourning month of Moharram when the Prince erected a large black tent in his garden as a place for prayer assemblies, the baker was always present, too, for he was very devout.

But devout in a special way, for the baker was a Sufi and belonged to a Sufi brotherhood, those religious organizations which follow the mystical tenets of Islam. Among those tenets especially revered by the baker was the belief that music and poetry of a mystical kind are aids along the Sufi Path to the House of God. For this reason, every week the baker hosted a gathering of poets and musicians. And he did this despite the fact that both his time and money were limited. Every day he was at his shop by four in the morning, returning home at noon for only an hour or two of food and sleep and then back again to his shop until eight or nine in the evening—except, of course, for those evenings devoted to the musicians and poets.

As for money, the baker's bread was famous in the city for its deliciousness and thus he did well. On the other hand, it cost him a pretty penny to provide for his guests, since he served only the finest of Indian teas, the best rice to be bought, the plumpest of chickens, the ripest of melons, yes, it took almost every penny he had.

All this expense was increased by the popularity of his evenings. Even those poets and musicians who had strayed from "the path" into the ways of the flesh (as musicians and poets are wont to do), finagled invitations, for the baker was loath to disappoint anyone whoever they might be, and he had also not forgotten his own dissolute youth and so forgave.

This popularity of the baker's evenings was not simply a matter of those plump chickens. There was, too, the appeal of the little house itself, its simple beauty and what some called its "emanation" of peace and love.

Guests, after stooping through the low door, found themselves on a stone walk in a tunnel of green stretching from the outside door to the house door, little and low as well. This tunnel was formed by a grape arbor and during the fruiting season it delighted the guests to see the grape clusters tied up in little bags of red felt, as though a flock of cardinals had taken up residence in the green thatch—though in fact the bags were there to protect the clusters from those very thieves, the birds. To either side of the arbor lay plantings of dwarf fruit trees interspersed with beds of roses, while the far walls were hung with jasmine vine. When the jasmine bloomed, the baker would gather the blossoms and put them on plates to perfume his rooms and please his guests.

Passing from this garden into the house, the guests found themselves in a spacious reception room. It was there that the baker stood to greet his guests, a small man, firm, clean, and brown, shaven-headed, a rather pointed face, high cheek bones, taunt skin, and little flitting, happy eyes—as if he saw comeliness in everything. He was always dressed the same; sandals, loose trousers of white cotton, a collarless blue shirt buttoned at throat and wrist. There he would stand—forever it sometimes seemed to him—engaging in the long Persian greetings.

From the reception room a broad doorway led into the assembly room. It was a domed chamber, a round skylight at the apex of the dome, baseboards of turquoise tile, small, crescent-shaped windows high in the white walls, a plain, red cotton carpet stretching down the room to a tiny fireplace. Above the fireplace there was a mural of a youth in the white wool gown of the early Sufis dancing in the hills above the city, his hands playing with golden stars spinning like heavenly tops in an azure sky.

Here then, in this beautiful room, the baker's evenings took place. First the baker, helped by some of the brothers, would serve the guests, who sat cross-legged in two long lines down the red carpet. The brothers placed before them great platters of chicken and saffron-steamed rice, the good lavash bread, and vase-sized glasses of *dugh*, a drink made of crushed rose petals, mint, and liquid yogurt. Supper completed, the brothers would bring ewers of perfumed water, basins, and towels that the guests might rinse their hands of the rich oils of the rice and the chicken.

These gross but nonetheless pleasing needs of the flesh satisfied, the remainder of the evening was devoted to the spirit. This began when the musicians took their instruments from felt cases, a flute, a drum, a three-stringed lute. With a tattoo from the drum the music commenced, the brothers slowly swaying in the drift of its melodies.

After a time it would be the turn of the poets to perform their love songs, sometimes recited, sometimes sung as sacred arias. By now the swaying of the assembled would have greatly increased and a few would have risen and moved to the carpet's center in a gyrating dance, their heads flung back, staring at the light in the dome's apex. Now and then, too, the plaintive cry of a soul seeking the ultimate union would mingle with the arias, the pluck of the lute, the shrill of the flute. For now the assembled, the baker, his brothers, even the wayward, were approaching the Sufi Way to the House of God and where the Sufi poet, Rumi, had written that they must "Knock at His door! Leave yourselves outside! And then go in!"

So in a crescendo of spiritual ecstasy the evening would end and the brothers, and even the wayward, would leave the baker's house refreshed with some kind of lightness, as if disembodied, no longer burdened.

III: THE PRINCE AND THE BAKER

Leaving his house one afternoon, the baker saw the Prince slowly proceeding down the lane. To the baker the Prince looked even more bent than usual and also his gait appeared unsteady. Instead of passing with his usual bow and muttered greeting, the baker stopped. So did the Prince. And they looked into each other's face. The baker saw grief, while the Prince saw clarity and some kind of brightness.

"Excellency," said the baker, "are you unwell?"

"The illness for which there is no cure," whispered the Prince. The baker nodded. "Ah yes, but it is only of the body. The soul does not waste away and never dies."

"But the soul may have its afflictions, too," said the Prince in an imperious voice, "its corruption!"

The baker looked more closely into the Prince's face and now saw more than grief, saw a soul on fire and he remembered Rumi: "…in the waters of Thy love, oh Lord…" and with that the baker took the Prince's arm, an audacity, but to the baker's mind the peril of the Prince's soul demanded it.

"Excellency, let me help you to your house…or better yet, come into my little garden and rest while I will bring you a lime sherbet with a sprig of mint."

There was no need for the Prince to stoop to pass through the baker's door, already weighed down as he was. The baker led him to a bench in a corner formed by the house and a wall and well canopied with jasmine vine, a snug and fragrant nook. After the Prince had settled himself on the bench, the baker touched his bowed shoulder and then went off to prepare the lime sherbet. When he returned he found the Prince's head nested in the jasmine vine, eyes closed, and there was almost a smile on his face. So began the friendship of the baker and the Prince.

These visits went on for several months, the Prince sitting on the nooked bench, the baker squatting on the ground at a respectable distance. The two often discussed neighborhood happenings, especially the scandals of which there were many and which both enjoyed. Of those old scandals with which the Prince had been charged, nothing was said, of course, nothing explicit that is, but the Prince, curious to know the baker's reaction, sometimes threw out little hints of the old charges in the delicate Persian way. The baker knew exactly what the Prince was about and that decorum absolutely forbade that a great prince and a lowly baker should openly discuss such matters between themselves. But the baker also sensed that these matters troubled the Prince, and so when the hint was dropped, the baker would shrug, and a clarity and brightness would come into his expression that touched the Prince like the balm of absolution.

More often than scandals and hints their visits were given over to the baker reciting Sufi poetry and sometimes playing to the Prince on his flute. The flute seemed to have a lulling effect, for often midway through a melody the Prince would close his eyes, nest his head in the jasmine vine, and begin to softly snore. The baker, after bringing a throw from the house to put over the Prince's knee, would hurry off to his shop. On his way he would stop to see Fatemeh—they were devoted old adversaries for they had haggled for years over the price of the bread—to give her the key to his door so that she might be with the Prince when he awoke.

As time passed the visits began to grow less frequent until finally Fatemeh called on the baker. The Prince, she told him, had grown so feeble, his gait so shambling, that he was no longer able to walk down the lane to the baker's garden. Other arrangements would have to be made.

The baker was in a quandary. For the Prince to visit him in his garden—neutral ground as it were—was one thing. For him, a simple baker, to presume to visit a great prince in his palace on a routine basis, was another, and to the baker's mind a straining of the bounds of propriety.

After long thought, the baker came up with a kind of solution. Every now and then he would send the Prince a gift, and to grace the gift he decided the bearers must be *shaheds*. A *shahed* is a beautiful youth. In the belief of some Sufis, a *shahed* is a reflection of the divine beauty. Now it happened the baker had a nephew and niece, both of great beauty. A young girl, of course, could not be a *shahed* for she might engender lust in the brothers rather than worship of the divine. But the Prince, however renowned for the lechery of his youth (and later too, for that matter), was now too old for lust and so there could be no harm in the baker enlisting his niece as a bearer of gifts. Indeed there could be some good in it for in addition to the sacred aspect of the matter, there was the belief in the native medicine that to the sick the sight of a beautiful face was tonic.

And so the visits began, the beautiful bearers with the baker's gifts; a jar of frankincense, a bowl of blooming narcissi bulbs, a white kitten, a spray from the jasmine vine, a cluster of the arbor grapes, a pitcher of that lime sherbet with a sprig of mint. The Prince, waking from the sleep that now more and more possessed him, saw with delight these gifts, gifts all the more precious to him for having come from the baker. And greatly pleasing him as well were the beautiful bearers, their presence filling his room with the air of spring, the beautiful boy reminding the Prince of the beauty of his own youth, the beautiful girl taking him back to the beautiful women he had loved.

Still, as the days passed, the Prince became less and less responsive to both the gifts and the beautiful youths. Finally one day in late autumn the baker's nephew came to tell the baker that on presenting the Prince with a little vial of attar of roses and which the baker had distilled from his own rose plantings, the Prince had barely sniffed at the vial and then drifted off again to sleep. The following day Fatemeh herself came to the baker. The Prince slept so much that she was hardly able to feed him. What could be done to rouse him?

The answer came to the baker a few nights later while entertaining his musicians and poets. He would send the musicians to play for the Prince. Perhaps the sacred melodies would rouse him from his sleep. The time the baker chose for this serenade was the fourteenth night, in the Islamic lunar calendar, the night of the full moon. Accordingly at about nine o'clock on the fourteenth, the musicians assembled in the courtyard below the Prince's rooms, the flute, the drum and the three-stringed lute. It was when the lute player began to sing, a high, ululating vibrato, that the Prince awoke. Fatemeh on her cot in the sitting room saw him in his nightshirt in the bedroom doorway, his hand out. She got up, took his hand, and led him to the balcony where he could look down on the courtyard and the musicians below. Though late in the autumn, it was a gentle night. An earlier shower had released the courtyard's perfumes, the orange trees, the jasmine, the soil itself and the enormous, copper moon, ridging high in the starry sky, cast a sheen over everything.

On seeing the Prince the musicians played a little salvo. He bowed and then waved his hand for them to continue. For some time he stood there, looking down, listening, Fatemeh holding his hand, his tears glistening in the moonlight.

It was early one evening, not long after the serenade, that Fatemeh came flying down the lane to tell the baker that the Prince was "leaving" and wished to see him. It happened that at the time the nephew and niece were with the baker and so they joined him and Fatemeh in hurrying to the Prince.

On reaching the house, they paused in the gallery, for the baker had never seen it before, the fourteen crystal chandeliers scattering their opalescence on the banners and flags, the armor, the glinting sabers—but there was no time to show him the wonderful music box and it was silent.

Upstairs they found the Prince white and still, stretched out on his bed, comatose. While loudly calling his name, Fatemeh tickled his ear with a feather, and in time his eyes opened and he saw the baker as well as the beautiful youths. The sight of all three seemed to give him strength and to everyone's astonishment he sat up in bed! The angel of death had come, he said, and he was ready to go, but first he wished to thank the baker for his gifts, the frankincense, the white kitten, the narcissi in bloom, the *shaheds*, the rest, but above all he wished to thank the baker for the greatest of his gifts…forgiveness. The baker smiled and the Prince saw in his face the clarity and brightness. The Prince then beckoned the baker to come closer, calling out his name; and the baker's name was Ali. Taking the baker's head between his two hands, the Prince drew his head down. The baker, knowing the Prince's wish, kissed the Prince on each cheek, the kiss of peace and the Prince smiled and folded his hands in his lap. And so the Prince died as he could never have imagined, a happy man.

THE WOMEN AND THE LADIES

THE WOMEN AND THE LADIES

Looking around apprehensively, the two women sat down. They were in the cocktail lounge of a luxury hotel in a Persian city known for its fine palaces and mosques. The cocktail lounge might have been anywhere—in Baltimore, for example, where the women lived. Still, the women were apprehensive. It was the waiters. "Too good looking," was the way Helen Black put it. The waiters were posted around the room, sometimes at attention, sometimes slouched, engaging—when they thought no one was looking—in quick horseplay. They looked like pirates; hook-nosed, black-eyed boys with fierce, beautiful faces.

"Yes, too good looking," said Helen Black again. "A man who is too good looking is in bad taste, like a woman who over-dresses."

Helen Black was a small, well-formed widow in her late forties with feathered gray-black hair and a snub nose that was like her girlhood looking out. She wore a knit suit, glasses on a cord, a good diamond on the blotched hand. Her friend, Mary Chapman, a divorcée, was younger, a blonde with big, tired eyes, white skin, and a mouth which had begun to thin and turn down. She had, as they say, "let herself go,"—in her red cashmere without a bra, a little blowzy.

The women rummaged in their enormous handbags and brought out cigarettes. After lighting up, they waved out their matches like brands, leaned back, and blew big funnels of smoke, giving sharp taps to their cigarettes on the glass rim of the ashtray.

"The poor women," Mary said. "I think I saw only two on the streets this morning who weren't veiled. I wonder what they wear under it—meant to ask the guide. But poor creatures. So curtailed."

"Oh, I don't know," said Helen. "After all, what else do they know?" A waiter came up.

"Screwdrivers," Mary said, looking a little below his eyes. Everyone in the country, it seemed to her, had the most peculiar eyes, a glisten to them as if they had just been weeping or were very happy, and a depth. It was the depth that disturbed. You couldn't look *at* their eyes but only, somehow, down into them, and it was too intimate.

"Yes, Madam. Two screwdrivers," the waiter said and turned away.

"Did you get a whiff of that?" Helen said. "Absolutely drenched in cologne. Must have spilled the bottle," she laughed.

"Queer, maybe," Mary mouthed, and then sat back, drawing on her cigarette.

The waiter gave the order to the bartender and then turned and leaned against the bar, looking down the lounge at the women. He was in his early twenties, a small, perfect body, a helmet of black hair, white teeth, and eyes which were the ideal of his race, almond shaped and tilted slightly downward in the dark, delicate face.

"The yellow one," he said as he moved his hand down his trouser-front and lightly, quickly cupped himself, "might not be bad."

"Ack," the bartender said, not looking up, busy with the drinks. "Yes, I know, some people have your taste—as a kind of

change, I suppose?" he looked up questioningly, then down
again. "But still I like a girl in bud, never yet have I seen anything over fifteen that really moved me."

"Well, you must try it," waiter said. "You see at their age," he
nodded toward the women, "what we have is for them precious
as the diamond." He began to gently bump against the bar. "Oh,
they will do anything, and with such passion! You and your fifteen year olds! Really, Abbas—you are so conservative."

"I am a content conservative," Abbas said, putting the screwdrivers on a tray. "Now give these to the ladies. Perhaps they
are thirsty."

"Poor ladies," the waiter said in another key, half sadness, half
humor, drawing a circle on the bar with his finger. "They
would enjoy themselves so much more this afternoon lying in
bed with us instead of walking around in the sun and looking
at those old buildings…I like the yellow one." He picked up the
tray and after looking down at himself to see that he was all in
order, he started out, walking like a dancer down to them.

He placed the little napkins and then the drinks. The
women sipped. He stood there. Helen Black looked up, wondering what he wanted, and then she smiled brightly and said:
"You make such good screwdrivers here."

"It is Madam's kindness." Then he turned to Mary Chapman. "And is the taste of yours good, Madam?"

"Why, yes, it's O.K.," she said.

"And what good English," Helen went on. He was such a
cordial boy; she liked him in spite of his flashy good looks.
"How ever did you learn it so well?"

"It is your kindness," he replied. "Also, I have a book and I
talk to the customers."

"Ah ha," Helen mused, her teeth on the rim of the glass. No
one said anything. The waiter bowed.

"Do you have any requests, Madam?"

"No, thank you very much," Helen replied. He turned away.

"Waiter," Mary called after him. He turned back. "Perhaps you could tell us. Someone said that the harem quarters at the River Palace are interesting to see. But it's not included in our tour. Is it worth seeing, worth going on our own?"

"It's empty," he replied.

"We know that. The palace hasn't been occupied for years. But I mean the place itself, the harem rooms. What's there to see anyway?"

He looked down at her. She was busy stirring her drink. "A pool and alcoves," he said, "and mirrors. I don't know. I have never been there, I have only heard."

"We find your city so interesting," Helen said. "We—by the way, what is your name? We Americans, you know, like to call people by their names."

"I am your servant, Jafar."

"Oh, I see. Well, anyway…Jafar…we do find your city so interesting, its glorious past, and your interesting customs, so different. The women, for example, in their veils. In fact, you know," she nodded at Mary, "my friend and I have a question. I wonder if we might ask you?"

"Any request, Madam…"

"Well, if you're sure you won't mind—then, it's this. Besides the veils your women wear, what other clothes, I mean in addition, what…?"

"Pardon?" he said, puzzled.

"They wear dresses then too, or…?"

"Oh yes, like you, Madam. Or, if they are young, the miniskirt."

"The miniskirt!" the women said in unison. "But what for," Helen asked, "since they are all covered up?"

"Why, for their husbands when they are at home," and he

tilted his head at each of them, his smile almost breaking into a laugh over this pleasant fact.

Mary Chapman, watching him charm Helen, so sure of himself, sat up and gave her cigarette a smart tap. With a concerned, challenging expression on her face, like a woman rising at a lecture to ask a question, she said: "There is something I'd like to ask you too, waiter."

"Any question," he said, smiling at her. But she looked away, playing again with her drink, and said:

"In the few days that my friend and I have been in your city we have seen so few women around, in the streets, in the shops, no women working, of course. They're at home, I suppose?"

"Yes," he said.

"Taking care of the house…?"

"Oh yes. They are very busy, the house, the children, the meals, and then, of course…they are our wives."

He sensed that he had said something wrong. He saw the older one's mouth go hard and her hand go inside her blouse and jerk at a strap. The yellow one was frowning. He looked away; it made her face ugly.

"But is that all?" Mary asked, jabbing out her cigarette. "Don't they have any diversions?"

"Oh yes," he said. "Of course. They go to the baths, sometimes for half the afternoon, taking fruit."

"Together?" Helen asked.

"Of course. They wouldn't go alone. And then they visit each other, sew, talk about the marriages, so much about the marriages…"

"The marriages?"

"Forced marriages," Mary said in a low voice to Helen.

"Deciding," he went on, "which girl is best for which boy and the other way around." He laughed. "They are very clever, those mothers, especially the mothers of sons, getting beautiful and good girls for their boys." He looked over their heads, across the room, as though thinking of other things.

"And that's all!" Mary said. "That's their amusement!"

"Yes. Of course they go on their picnics and then there's the mosque. They like that very much, to listen to the preachers and pray."

"My God," Helen said, turning the big diamond on her finger.

The little pig, Mary thought, staring at the perfect brown body and at the face, like a face from some lewd and beautiful frieze.

"I'm afraid," Helen said, "it's all a little difficult for us to conceive. You see, in our country women have such a wide range of interests—and then they are so free. My friend and myself, for example. We travel, see the world. And at home we are active in so many things, community projects, we take courses at the university—do you understand?" He nodded, looking puzzled again. "Golf, why we even make pots, ceramics, you know. Of course we aren't married, now. But even when we were married we had this freedom, this freedom to do what we wanted. Your women on the other hand—but then I suppose they are happy in their way... After all, it's a different culture, isn't it." She looked at her watch. "What do you say, Mary? Time for another drink?"

When the waiter went off, Helen leaned forward. "He's rather sweet, isn't he? Student, I suppose, summer work, poor child."

"Why poor child? There is brass in that poor child if you ask me, something—I don't know if it's the way he uses his eyes or what—but anyway, a certain cheek."

He was back. The drinks had come much faster this time.

"Well, waiter," Mary said, "to continue our little discussion, that is if you don't mind. You know that we are here, after all, to understand your country."

"Yes Madam," he said, looking down into her eyes with a half-smiling stare, playing with one of the lower buttons on his shirt.

"Those things my friend was talking about," she said, glancing at him and then instantly away, for it was as if she had touched hot iron. "Those things," she went on, her voice breaking slightly, "that women in our country are free to do. Don't you think that your women would like some of that freedom too?"

"I don't understand," he said, still staring at her, not interested in what she was saying.

"Well, is just the house, going to the baths, visiting—praying, I think you said—are those things really all that interesting for them, that broadening?"

"There is only the day's time. Their husbands, their children, their parents, their friends. There isn't time for the things you mentioned and anyway they wouldn't be interesting for our ladies, at least for our ordinary, usual ladies. Our great ladies, of course, are doctors, lawyers, engineers, they go to our parliament, but most of our ladies, like most of our men, are ordinary and they do those ordinary things that I told you. No, the things you mentioned would not be interesting for our ladies."

"I wonder," Mary said. "I wonder. Perhaps," she laughed, "perhaps the men in your country, like the men in mine, do not know their ladies very well." And then the question occurred to her. She felt like a teacher who has found the question which will show the student how ignorant he is and so be the beginning of knowledge. "Jafar," she said, seriously, gently, "do you have a wife?" And as she said it she began to construct in her mind the phrasing of her answer, how, when he married, he would understand what she was talking about if he tried to be really sensitive to his wife's real needs…and then his answer came through to her.

"Oh yes. Two."

"Two what?" she said.

"Two wives."

She felt as if she had been slapped by this preening boy. She gave him a quick look, half anger, half hurt. And he looked back, teasing her with his eyes.

"Oh, Jafar!" said Helen, laughing. "You are incorrigible. Well, let's try it another way. But you must think about this before you answer, really think about it." She shook her finger at him. "You must be truthful. What do you think your wife— your wives—want most, like most in the world?"

"Me," he said very simply, looking down.

Mary threw back her head and laughed, hoarsely, almost as if she were coughing. Her breasts rolled under the red cashmere and Jafar, watching, imagined laying his head between them.

"Well, Mary," Helen said, "there is no doubt about it. Here the male ego is in excellent shape. My word!" Then she looked quickly up at Jafar. "And for you the most important thing…?"

"Them…my ladies. Surely in your country it's the same, ladies are the most important thing, surely in all our world there is nothing more important, more wonderful."

"But that," said Mary, "puts us in a special category."

"What?" he said.

"I mean it makes us special and different."

"Yes," he said.

She looked away up the room. Really, what was the use? He was a child. She smiled up at him, patiently. "You know, Jafar, what you are? You're a selfish child," and she tapped her cigarette.

How he liked her now. She was smiling, her mouth turned up, and teasing him and that was good. "Madam," he said, "please accept a thousand apologies but you are wrong. I am a man, and Madam's slave." He made a low, mocking bow, looking up at her from under his brows, his glance for an instant circling her breasts.

"And gallantry too," Helen said, "is in pretty good shape." Then she showed her watch to Mary. "If we want to get some lunch and catch that tour we had better get a move on. Jafar, bring the check please."

"Yes, Madam." And he went off up the lounge, swinging his shoulders and once turning his head so that they might see his profile.

"Oh my lovely one!" he said to the bartender. "Her breasts, Abbas! If only she didn't talk so much or said different things, my lovely yellow one."

"You are mad," said the barman.

Jafar leaned over the bar. "I want to give her something that will please her."

"Be careful!" said the bartender. "That 'something' of yours will get you into trouble and you'll be back slaving in a teahouse."

"No, no. You don't understand. Not that—it's impossible, too risky. No, what I want to give her is the wink."

"The wink?"

"Yes, the wink. The pinch is out. Some foreign ladies, the Italians, the French, like the pinch but not the American ladies. They like the wink."

"The wink? What are you talking about?"

"The wink of the eye. I have seen the foreign gentlemen do it, here in this bar, do it to the American ladies and they like it. I know, it's very curious why they prefer the wink to the pinch, but anyway they do, and since I want to please my yellow one, that's what I shall give her."

"Give her the check," said the bartender. "They are looking

this way, poor ladies."

Jafar put the check on the tray and taking his time walked down the lounge. "Forgive me ladies. Our bartender," he clucked his tongue, "is so slow."

Mary opened her purse. She was careful to add only a ten percent tip; anything more might be misinterpreted. She held out the money to him, determined to look him in the eye. He looked back, his lids a little lowered, his eyes smiling but not quite focused, and suddenly from nowhere, fighting it, she felt deeply lulled and pleasured. Shaking her head as if she were in a daze, she said: "Here's the money; take it."

"Well, Jafar," Helen said, "we have enjoyed talking to you so much. It's really been so interesting."

"You are so kind," Jafar replied. "You have honored us so much. And we shall remember you."

The women got up. "Oh, by the way," Helen said, inclining her head to him, "do say hello to your ladies for us, will you? Tell them two American women wish them the best of health and happiness."

Then Helen and Mary slung on their enormous handbags and started out. At the door Mary turned back. She wanted one more look at him. He was there, by the table, facing her and as she gazed at him she saw the lid bat slowly down across the tilted almond eye. Guiding her voice, fearing that it might break, she called out to him, "Jafar, Jafar." And then she turned and she and Helen left.

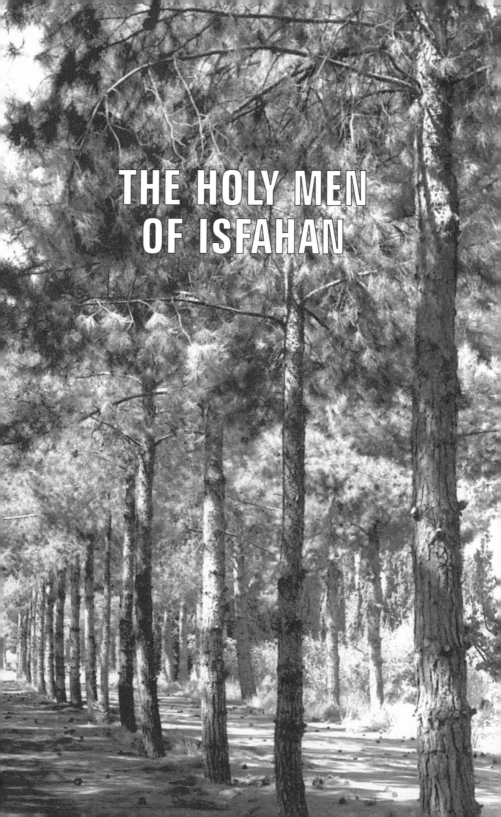

THE HOLY MEN
OF ISFAHAN

THE HOLY MEN OF ISFAHAN

Norad Karkerian, Archbishop of the Armenian Church of the Roman Rite, walked from his palace, down through the garden, to the riverbank. There he entered a columned pavilion and sat down in a chair whose armrests ended in carved lions' heads. Wrapping his skirts around his legs—for the damp autumn wind was blowing from the river—he took out his beads, closed his eyes, and began to pray, waiting for the others.

The palace, built of whitewashed mud-brick, looked like a little fort; square, flat-roofed, at one corner a two-story tower which had settled a bit and so was aslant. A long grape arbor separated the palace from the cathedral. The cathedral was also small and built of mud-brick but in the Western style, two towers and a nave. These towers, too, were not quite straight. The garden which sloped from the palace and cathedral to the riverbank was in fact an orchard of mulberry trees. They had not nourished silkworms for many years but there were still vestments from that time hanging in the vestry.

The Archbishop's church had been founded by Jesuits in the seventeenth century, the Jesuits in Isfahan on some embassy from a Western power to the Shah of Persia. The Jesuits' purpose in founding the church had been to win the Shah's Armenian subjects back to Rome from the Eastern church. Their efforts had not been greatly successful. The Archbishop's see, which stretched from the western borders of Turkey to Borneo, comprised only a few hundred souls, most of these in India, descendants of Armenian merchants who had gone there to trade.

The Archbishop had been born in Isfahan, or more specifically Julfa, the Armenian quarter of the city. When a boy he was sent to the Armenian College in Venice and from there he had gone to Rome to take holy orders. Possessing a talent for music, he had in time become Vatican choirmaster. In his eightieth year he was retired and as a reward for his labors made archbishop of his native church.

"Wake up, wake up! They're coming!" cried Maria Halkian at the pavilion door—for the Archbishop had fallen asleep. Maria Halkian was an unfrocked nun and the Archbishop's housekeeper. On his return to Isfahan to take up his duties, the Archbishop found irregular practices at the convent and had closed it down. Maria Halkian, alone of the nuns, received his compassion, for she was without family and destitute. After imposing a severe penance upon her, he brought her to the palace to keep house for him.

Maria Halkian, now in her seventies, was a stump of a woman, always bundled in black and still wore her veil—at this point no more than a rag. This rag and her nose reminded the Archbishop of some mummified nuns he had once seen in a convent crypt in Siena. The matter of her nose was that there was almost no flesh on it, a little scoop of bone, the ravages of syphilis, everyone knew, "inherited," the charitable said. Another disagreeable feature of Maria Halkian was that she stank of garlic and seldom washed. The resulting effluvium was for His Grace a cross but like the others—no choir, the dampness of the palace, the absence of pasta—he offered it up.

Rising from his chair, the Archbishop took Maria's arm with one hand, his staff in the other, and started up the willow-lined alley which led through the orchard to the palace. His guests were approaching from the other end. In front, and according to protocol, was the Imam Jumeh, chief Muslim cleric of the city. Behind him and abreast, again according to protocol, came the Anglican Bishop of Persia (Isfahan was his seat), the Chief Rabbi of Isfahan, and the Archimandrite of the Armenian Church of the Eastern rite.

The Imam Jumeh, on seeing the Archbishop, seemed to hop and then dipped forward, his gown dragging behind on the ground. The Archbishop likewise hurried his steps until, within speaking distance, he stopped, raised his head high as though addressing the heavens, and said in a loud but quavering voice, "My brothers in God." All bowed.

On reaching the pavilion it took some time for the divines to seat themselves for protocol demanded that the Imam Jumeh should do so first. This he refused with many professions of unworthiness. Finally, of course, he did but only after elaborate apologies which took some time as well. At last all were seated in the lion-headed chairs, leaning forward, bowing to one another.

The Imam Jumeh, seated to the Archbishop's right, had been born of peasant parents in one of the poorer upriver villages. The landlord of the village, seeing promise, had sent him off as a boy to study theology in the holy city of Qom. There he had not distinguished himself as a scholar, but on the other hand he was seen by his mentors as a true friend of God. It was this together with something exceptionally pleasing about his person which led to his subsequent rise.

Indeed all agreed on the Imam's absolute saintliness. All agreed as well on his absolute incompetence. After all, his duties as chief mullah of the city required some administrative ability; he had none. Requests made of him, if answered at all, could take several years in the granting—all this because of his general muddle-headedness. Yet he was much loved, all wanting to kiss his hand. Only the most ill-natured condemned him for his love of fatty foods. This was not for reasons of health—indeed it was considered the cause of his robust good health—but rather because it was judged that the money spent upon these foods might better have been given to the poor.

Like the Archbishop, the Imam Jumeh was now in his eighties, a tiny man with the face of a pretty child, red-cheeked and—unusual in a Persian—blue-eyed. A face with some kind of gleam or luminosity to it, his holiness, some said, the fatty foods, said others. In the Archbishop's judgement it was due to the simple fact that he was always smiling, a rather foolish smile, he sometimes thought, but he tried not to judge.

The Imam Jumeh now sat on a red velvet cushion with gold tassels, placed in his chair out of deference but also to boost him a bit, and this cushion, together with his attire—a green turban, a midnight blue soutane, a camel-hair cloak of the palest fawn—made him look like an exotic little bird perched on some gorgeous flower. The impression was strengthened by his habit of jerking rather than turning his head and this with great frequency as though he would miss nothing of God's glorious creation.

If the Imam Jumeh was a twitchy little bird of exotic hue, the divine to his right was a large, immobile crow. This was Roger Kent, the Anglican Bishop of Persia, black-gaitered, black-coated, only the thinnest piping of purple around his collar, tall and stooped, a long neck, a bald, egg-shaped head and an expression of permanent dolor upon his face.

The Bishop by his early training had been an engineer and as such he had been sent out many years before to supervise repairs on the Taj Mahal. On his way he stopped in Julfa—one of the few Christian communities between Turkey and India—and there met the then Bishop of Persia's daughter, with whom he fell in love. After completing his work on the Taj Mahal, Kent took holy orders at Oxford and then returned to Isfahan and married the Bishop's daughter. (It was said that the Persian bishopric descended in the female line. Bishop Kent's predecessor and father-in-law had himself married his predecessor's daughter while Bishop Kent's only child, a daughter, was now being courted by a young curate who would, of course, marry her and in the fullness of time become himself the Anglican Bishop of Persia.)

Bishop Kent's see was much smaller than the Archbishop's—which, after all, comprised about a quarter of the globe—and even smaller in the number of its communicants; a few aging British spinsters who did good works, most of them in the mission hospital the Bishop maintained. For the Bishop had made no converts. The majority of the people of the city, 99.9 percent Muslim, respected the Bishop and his good works—sometimes even leaving him money in their wills—but they would not have dreamt of exchanging Mohammad for Christ, except perhaps as a temporary expedient. Only in one, long ago instance was hostility expressed toward the Bishop and his church. A rich fanatic had caused a row of public water closets to be built opposite the gate to the Bishop's house and these with their attendant cesspits did cause offense, literally a stench in the Bishop's nose.

In any event, the Bishop had to be content with a church of small membership. But he had faith which is everything and it may be too that he had come to the conclusion of many elderly missionaries; that in the end it didn't much matter what one's faith was, so long as one loved God.

To the right of the Bishop sat Abraham Garbade, the chief

rabbi of the city. Rabbi Garbade was a massive and powerful man with a voice like a drum and a heavy apron of glossy red beard which was the envy of every man in Isfahan. He was the descendant of a long line of Isfahan rabbis—for Isfahan, with Baghdad, had once been a great center of rabbinical studies—and before that of a Russian family who after several generations of traveling the fairs of the Middle East with a troop of performing bears, had finally settled in Isfahan. Rabbi Garbade was perhaps a throwback to these roving ancestors, for when a young man, he decided to continue his rabbinical studies in what he then considered some of the world's more exotic cities: Paris, Rome, London, Vienna, Budapest, Istanbul, and Cairo. In late middle-age, and after some thirty years in these great cities, Rabbi Garbade returned to Isfahan with an Alexandrian wife, many children, and much knowledge of the world.

Of the divines gathered on this afternoon in the Archbishop's pavilion, only Rabbi Garbade and the Imam Jumeh could be considered as more than acquaintances. This had come about because the Imam's mosque, the Friday mosque, which is to say the cathedral mosque of the city, stood in the middle of the Jewish quarter and thus it was that the Imam and the Rabbi often encountered each other in the lanes and where they engaged, first on one leg, then on another, in long, theological disputations.

Finally there was Valarian, Archimandrite of the Armenian Church of the Eastern rite, and the only stranger among them. The Armenians had come to Isfahan in the sixteenth century, brought by Shah Abbas the Great to ornament his capital, for they were known to be fine craftsmen. Abbas built them a small but beautiful cathedral, gave them a charter of religious freedom, and they had been there ever since—though a few of them, as noted earlier, were seduced away to

Rome by the Jesuits.

The center of this church of the Eastern rite was Yerevan, capital of what at this time was Soviet Armenia. Before the Russian Revolution this caused no problem, but following the Revolution it did, for the archimandrites sent from Yerevan tended more toward political than religious proselytization. Finally the Shah had put his foot down; the Armenians of the Eastern rite were told they must get their archimandrites from somewhere else. In the end they had been obliged to accept a man from Beirut, the present archimandrite.

Except in one respect, Valarian was an unknown quantity for he had only recently arrived in Isfahan. There was not even gossip about him—which in Isfahan was remarkable. It was certainly true that he looked as an archimandrite should. He was tall, displayed a fine beard, and had the face of an eagle, a grand nose, and angry eyes. It was true as well that his garb was acceptable; a gown of black shot-silk girdled by a scarlet sash, a flared black hat of good felt and a staff larger, longer, and more ornately crowned in silver than that of the Archbishop. And, of course, he was indisputably Armenian and of the Eastern rite. But he was a Levantine. Persians of whatever faith tend to distrust the sea and anyone connected with it, and perhaps because it is associated with Arabs. In short, there were questions about Valarian, Archimandrite of the Armenian Church of the Eastern rite.

After a suitable period of silence, all nodding to one another, the Archbishop grasped the lion heads and said in his quavering voice: "My brothers in God. You honor me, to have left your busy day, to have come here to your poor servant in his poor house."

Each raised a protesting hand as if not deserving of the Archbishop's compunction on their behalf. Except for Bishop Kent who dryly said: "You are too kind."

"Well," the Archbishop wrapped his soutane more tightly around his legs, "as you may or may not know, our feast of the Katchurian approaches."

"When you all jump in the river," the Rabbi rumbled, and the Imam smiled.

The Archbishop frowned. "Not exactly. We choose ten of the most stalwart youths of our community and then," he flapped his hand at the river, "they assemble on the riverbank, and then as you may know—well!" The Archbishop leaned back and thumped his staff on the floor. "Our brother in God, John, the Bishop of Rome, has in his last pastoral enjoined upon us to act in the *ecumenical* mode." The Archbishop used the English word, for the divines were conversing in Persian and the word does not exist in Persian. It was no doubt for this reason that the Imam, looking more confused than ever, twitched his head from one to the other, seeking explanation.

"An absolutely splendid idea, if I may say so, this ecumenical business," said Bishop Kent. "You are aware, of course, that I went on pilgrimage Christmas last to Jerusalem. And for the first time we Anglicans were given permission by the—the factotums, or whatever you call them, anyway the so-called authorities," he laughed, "of the Church of the Holy Sepulcher, permission to conduct services, there at that place." The Bishop paused and looked at each of his brothers in turn. "And where do you think they put us? *On the roof!* Yes, I am ashamed to say, profoundly ashamed, if I may say so, yes, on the *roof.*" The dolor on the Bishop's face deepened.

The Imam raised his hand and in a voice which had earned him the nickname of "the squeak," he said: "I cannot think our doorkeeper would be so inhospitable and if so I am deeply grieved."

There was an embarrassed silence. All knew that when Saladin the Great returned the church to the Christians in 1192 it was with the stipulation that the keys of the church would always remain in Muslim hands. And indeed to this day the keys are held by a Muslim doorkeeper whose station is in the porch of the church and it is he who each morning and evening opens and shuts the door. A little reminder. And the Imam remembered, as did his Christian brothers. Bishop Kent took out a large bandanna handkerchief and spat into it. On the face of the Archimandrite there came a look of great hauteur and the angry eyes looked even angrier. But he did not speak.

He could not. It has been said that there was only one thing known with certainty about the Archimandrite. This was that he was intemperate of speech. Recently, for example, he had spoken rashly by comparing Isfahan unfavorably with Beirut and in no uncertain terms, "a slum," he had said of the former. In contrition he had imposed upon himself a penance of silence, twenty-one days of it. This was only day four and so all he could do was look; thus the hauteur and the angrier-than-ever eyes.

The Bishop, replacing his handkerchief, replied: "No Holiness," he bowed to the Imam, "it was not your doorkeeper. It was the church's so-called council—Greeks, Romans, Copts, Ethiopians, Nestorians, all that crew."

The conversation had taken an acrimonious turn and the Archbishop was about to lead it in a more pacific direction when there arose from the high grasses of the riverbank the tinkle and pop of a tambourine. The divines, all frowning, turned in their chairs to see fifty yards or so down the riverbank a man in a black hat with a rose in his teeth, arms flailing, doing a pirouette.

To the Archbishop's profound embarrassment, this stretch of the riverbank served as a resort for the toughs of the city who would repair there on a sunny afternoon to drink and dance—

and other things the Archbishop tried not to think about.

"Disgusting," Bishop Kent said, turning back. "And I suppose they have a boy with them."

"Sodomites," thundered the Rabbi. "In the cities of the West which I have known, such persons would be arrested. But not, of course, in Cairo or Istanbul, not to mention Isfahan," the Rabbi added with a leer. The implication was clear; only in Islam was such sinfulness tolerated.

"But my dear Rabbi," said the Imam, "to bring a girl would cause scandal. And anyway doesn't your St. Augustine say, 'Love and do what you like'?"

"He's not *my* St. Augustine," replied the Rabbi, very much in a huff. "He belongs to them," and he gestured toward the Christians.

"Well, God knows best," lamely concluded the Imam.

"St. Paul—" began the Bishop.

"And I understand," interrupted the Rabbi, turning to the Bishop, "that it is rife in your public schools."

"What is rife in our public schools, if I may ask?"

"Sodomy."

Bishop Kent closed his eyes and turned his head away, declining to answer such an absurd charge. The Archimandrite, who from his shifting about in his chair, was having difficulty in restraining his tongue, had to content himself with a glower and by making the sign of the cross. Then abruptly Bishop Kent returned to the field, though this time turning his guns on the Imam.

"And the drink. That at least I have been given to understand is forbidden in Islam."

For once there was no smile on the Imam's face but instead an aggrieved little pout. "But it is you who make it," he cried, "you Christians and," he turned to the Rabbi, "you Jews. You who make it and sell it. Why, every drink shop in the city is owned by one or the other of your people. No Muslim would engage in such a traffic."

"You just drink it," the Rabbi growled.

"A minority, a minority," the Imam said, turning to the Archbishop with saddened eyes, as if pleading with the Archbishop to rescue him from the rancor of the Rabbi and the Bishop, as well as the disapproving gaze of the Archimandrite.

"My brothers," began the Archbishop, "to return to the Katchurian." Then he stopped. Maria was shuffling toward them with a tray of cakes and tea, and for the Imam a bowl of hard-boiled eggs and oranges. What to serve the Imam had been a problem.

The Archbishop could understand it, rationally, but nonetheless it irked him, this Muslim belief that Christians and Jews, and all they touched, were unclean. Yes, he could understand that in the time of Mohammad, when everyone was quite filthy, the Prophet had seen fit to institute elaborate and extensive ablutionary laws—the washing of all the extremities before the daily calls to prayer and from head to foot following intercourse, the latter meaning that Muslims spent half their lives in the bathhouses, or so it seemed to the Archbishop. But now everyone bathed—he brushed the thought of Maria from his mind—and thus it appeared to the Archbishop that the prohibition should be dropped. However, the Imam, like the rest of the Muslim hierarchy, was a stick-in-the-mud and that was that.

So the problem of what to serve the Imam. At the last moment the obvious came to the Archbishop's mind. On high Muslim holy days it had always been his custom to send the Imam a gift basket of eggs and oranges, and from both of which the Imam could, of course, peel the uncleanness off.

However old hat, he had decided the same would have to do for this occasion.

Maria was now among them, stooping low with her tray before the Imam who daintily plucked an egg from the bowl, though his eyes were on the pistachio and honey cakes. The others served, Maria retired and there occurred that oddity of Persian etiquette which requires that discourse be periodically punctuated by intervals of silence. This silence, except for the sounds of mastication, now descended. Even the tambourine had ceased. Then suddenly there came into this silence from the tall grasses of the riverbank a long, drawn-out ululation, half cry, half moan. The divines all began talking at once.

The Rabbi's voice, deeper and stronger, prevailed. "Now what about this Katchurian or whatever you call it?"

The Archbishop, his eyes downcast, smoothed the soutane over his knees. "It's an ancient rite among us, long in abeyance here in Isfahan but now," he looked up, smiling at the others, "I have thought to revive it!"

"Yes, but what is it?" the Rabbi persisted.

The Archbishop raised his hand. "Patience, my dear Rabbi, patience. All will be revealed."

"Is it from Rome?" Bishop Kent asked with a meaningful glance at the Archimandrite. The Archimandrite raised both hands, palms outward, as though to ward off some profanation. Before the Archbishop could answer, Husayn, the hunchbacked garden boy, limped into the pavilion, on his arm a basket filled with little bouquets of dog roses which, kneeling before each of the divines in turn, he offered to them. When he reached the Rabbi, the Rabbi leaned forward and touched his hump.

"Blessed is God," he intoned, "for He hath created diversity."

"Blessed is God," the others all replied in chorus.

The Bishop, his nose in the flowers, returned to the field. "From Rome, I asked?"

The Archbishop could not restrain himself. "You who have left Rome," be bowed to the Bishop and the Archimandrite— the latter's face now very red, "ascribe everything to Rome. You must remember, as I am sure you do, that we Armenians are the oldest of the Christian peoples," he sat back and grasped his staff, "and we have our ancient traditions of which the Katchurian is one."

"I daresay," the Bishop replied. "I only ask because your bonds, after all, are to Rome." He paused, then coughed. "Bonds from which, if I may say so, the Archimandrite and myself are free." He coughed again, a very dry little cough. And for the first time there appeared on the face of the Archiman- drite a smile.

The Imam, shaking the egg shells off his soutane onto the floor, turned to the Archbishop. "There are so many cults among you Christians, this rite, that rite, another rite—I find it most confusing. But the thing which confuses me most, puzzles me most I should say, is why in your cult, my dear Archbishop, you are forbidden to marry! I find it—forgive me—most shocking, against the nature which God has ordained. The rest of us here…" he jerked about on the red velvet cushion, nod- ding to each of the others, "have wives. Indeed," he shielded his face with his hand and giggled, "I have three."

It was true. The Rabbi had his Alexandrian, still quite beauti- ful in the Levantine way. Mrs. Kent was in no way beautiful but she was imposing, being almost twice the size of the Bishop in both height and breadth. As for the Archimandrite, he was now a widower but at least he had had a wife—and she too a great beauty, or at least so he claimed. Only the Archbishop had been chaste through all the years of his long life. Raising his head high with pride, the Archbishop answered.

"You see, Holiness, we of Rome who are in service to God believe that we should be in service to no one else except in the general sense, to our flock that is."

The Imam stared at him for a long moment. Then ducking his head, splaying his fingers across his face, though observing the Archbishop between his fingers, he giggled again.

"Well, you have your Maria."

The Rabbi guffawed. The Archbishop flushed. It was not the accusation itself but the suggestion that he was obliged to content himself with the mummified nun when there were plenty of Armenian ladies who would have been only too happy to receive his favors.

In general, it was not going at all as he had planned, acrimonious for one thing, now turned salacious as well. Where was peace, the peace of God? Bishop Kent's querulous voice interrupted his thoughts.

"What I do not understand, Imam, is why you must have three?"

"Yes, excessive," the Rabbi said, shifting from one haunch to the other.

A boil on his bottom, I hope, thought the Archbishop, and then said to himself a quick mea culpa, striking his breast.

"Excessive," the Imam repeated. "Not at all," and he gave a quick, cocky little toss to his head. "For as you yourself just said, dear Rabbi, 'Blessed is God for He hath created diversity.'"

"Well, there is diversity and diversity," said the Rabbi, "speaking of which listen. And look."

For the tinkle of the tambourine had begun again, accompanied by a rhythmic clapping and the divines, all turning, saw in the high grasses of the riverbank a young boy pirouetting, in his hand a tambourine, on his head a red funnel-shaped hat looped with spangles, glinting in the sun.

"One of yours, I should think, Rabbi," drawled the Bishop.

"You assume," said the Rabbi.

They did. From the beginning of time the dancing boys of the city, as well as the minstrels, had come from the ranks of the Jews, since music was forbidden to Muslims.

"And what if he is one of ours," said the Rabbi, shifting haunches again. "It is not sinful for us to play instruments and dance." He turned to the Imam. "It is you who sin when you listen and watch!"

The Imam cast his eyes down and covered his ears with the palms of his hands.

"I do not watch or listen, if I can help it, and I enjoin my people not to do so either. May God…"

"It's not the dancing as such, Rabbi," interrupted Bishop Kent. "It's what it so often leads to, or so I am informed."

The Rabbi half rose from his chair, the great red apron of beard flaring out. "How dare you!" his voice boomed like a cannon at the Bishop. "Our Jewish boys are pure. Not like your public schools." The Rabbi sank back in his chair, patting his beard back into place, and looked at each of the others with eyes angrier even than the Archimandrite's.

"My brothers, my brothers, please," the Archbishop said. "We must be here in peace despite our different ways."

The others said nothing and to the Archbishop's relief the customary interval of silence descended. The Archbishop took out his rosary. The Bishop closed his eyes. The Rabbi stroked his beard. The Imam nibbled at another egg. Even the tambourine had ceased. There was only the stroking, the nibbling, the click of the beads. These, too, finally stopped. Peace. Then the Archimandrite loudly, and at some length, broke wind.

The Archbishop could not restrain himself. "My dear Archimandrite, you have broken your vow of silence."

All laughed, even the Archimandrite, rocking back and forth in the lion-headed chairs, and from then on their gathering took a happier turn.

The laughter went on at such length that several black-hatted heads, as well as the spangled red one, appeared above the tall grasses of the riverbank, all turned in the divines' direction. Finally, the laughter subsided, all blowing their noses, wiping their eyes, settling themselves back in their chairs and wagging their heads at one another and smiling at the wonderful joke. Then the Archimandrite spoke, the accent foreign, and the inflection Levantine, a kind of wheedling sing-song, like someone trying to sell something—though for all that a voice of power.

"Brethren. I have, as you say, spoken, however inadvertently." The Archimandrite smiled into his beard and there was from the others a chorus of titters. "And having spoken, as it were, I shall speak again and tomorrow renew my vow. Now!" he grasped his pectoral cross, "I wish to tell you that we, too, of the Eastern rite observe the Katchurian, an ancient rite among we Armenians, established long before Rome strayed." The Archimandrite bowed to the Archbishop. "Still my brother and I share this holy observance."

"Well," said the Rabbi, smiling, "perhaps then and between the two of you, you can tell us what it is." The Imam and the Bishop nodded in agreement.

The Archbishop grasped his staff, thumping it softly on the floor. "You are right. We must get on with this. Now: the Katchurian commemorates our Lord's baptism in the waters of the Nile." He paused, trying to see the Imam and the Rabbi out of the corner of his eye. "And his manifestation as the son of God!"

The Rabbi flapped his beard while with trembling hands the

Imam covered his eyes. The Christians crossed themselves. Then the Archbishop bowed to the Imam and the Rabbi.

"I hope I do not give offense. It is our belief."

"Jesus," said the Rabbi with unusual gentleness, "was a good Jew, a good man." He paused. "But no more, no less," he added with a frown.

The Imam put down his half peeled orange and pointed to the sky. "There is only one God, one only, no two or three…this 'trinity' of yours. Shame. Your Christ was a great prophet whom we honor but certainly no god."

All leaned back in their chairs, knowing that this question of the divinity of Christ was a subject hopeless to pursue, this theological knot which however much they picked at it in their different ways would never come untied.

"Well, to go on," the Archbishop said. "As I mentioned earlier, we shall choose ten of our stalwarts…"

"Twelve," interrupted the Archimandrite.

"Ten I do believe."

"Twelve. It has always been twelve."

"Make it eleven," said the Rabbi, lifting the afflicted haunch.

"In any event," the Archbishop continued, "our young stalwarts will gather on the riverbank and then I—" he glanced at the Archimandrite, "then we, I should say, will cast a crucifix into the waters. At this the young men will dive in…"

"As I said earlier," the Rabbi interrupted, "you all jump in the river."

"Yes, my dear Rabbi, but not all of us. Just the young men. And they will seek to rescue the crucifix from the water and he who succeeds, the hero, will be garlanded with flowers by a delegation of our young ladies."

"They must be matrons, not virgins," the Archimandrite said with severity.

"Whatever. Then of course refreshments will be served, a gala, a celebration." The Archbishop gave a strong thump to his staff. "It will be lovely but only a loveliness complete if you will all honor us with your presence," he paused, "and thus will our brother, the Bishop of Rome, be gratified to hear of the winds of the ecumenical spirit blowing through our beloved Isfahan and cleansing us of our differences—at least for one afternoon." The Archbishop leaned far back in his chair, beaming at each of his brothers in turn.

No one spoke. It was for the Imam to first respond. Before he could do so, Maria appeared with another tray of refreshments.

"Just this one time," said the Imam, snatching up a pistachio and honey cake. "I'll wash out my mouth when I get home. Now my dear Archbishop…" he paused, his mouth clogged with cake. They waited. "Now," he finally went on, "I am truly most honored by your most kind invitation. However, I regret to say that there are certain obstacles."

The Archbishop had feared there would be certain, if not many obstacles, but he was determined to compromise, insofar as possible. "In the spirit of God's peace may they be overcome," he said, reaching toward but not touching the Imam's hand.

The Imam gulped down the last of the cake, wiping his mouth with the sleeve of his soutane. "Maria, may I compliment you on your sweets."

The old woman looked at him with horror—eating unclean food in public and thanking her to boot. "To the matter at hand." He turned to the Archbishop. "My dear Archbishop, may I ask how the young men will be clad. As you know, the law of Islam requires that the body be fully clothed from head to toe so as not to incite lust. Surely even your own creed would frown on your maidens, your matrons too I might add, gazing upon these young men in their near nakedness!"

"Let them wear dressing gowns," the Bishop yawned.

"They don't have dressing gowns," the Archbishop replied with an asperity he at once regretted.

"Drape them in sheets," the Rabbi said. "Or don't you Armenians use sheets," he added, laughing.

"Yes, and we wash them too," the Archimandrite growled, a veiled reference to the fact that the Isfahan Jews were not known for their cleanliness.

Sheets. The Archbishop and the Bishop looked at one another. Sheets were what Muslims wore when on pilgrimage to Mecca. But there was no way out.

"Well, let it be sheets," the Archbishop said, his voice sinking in disappointment. Then he brightened. "So all is settled. You agree?" He clapped his knees. "You will all be here to help us celebrate our holy Katchurian?"

The Imam shook his head. "There is the matter of the cross."

"The cross!" the three Christians cried in unison, their voices strident as a battle cry.

"The cross," the Imam repeated. He turned to the Rabbi. "We have discussed this many times before my dear Rabbi and you know we cannot accept it, this little fib you Jews have told about Jesus, the Christians' great prophet and whom as I have said we Muslims also much revere. As Mohammad—blessed be his name—has told us, God would never let such an end befall one of his great prophets, this crucifixion." He wrinkled his nose. "It is an abomination."

"Lie!" the word roared from the Rabbi like a terrible wind. "Lie, lie, you say we lie!"

The Archbishop stood up. "My brothers, peace, peace, I implore you, remember God."

"Such a to-do," Bishop Kent drawled, crossing his gaitered legs.

It was what the Archbishop had most feared, this question of the cross, knowing that both the Imam and the Rabbi would strongly object, the one believing it had never existed, the other in his heart of hearts believing it to have been fit punishment for a man who had blasphemed by calling himself the son of God. Oh Holy Father, the Archbishop silently prayed, bring us to peace, let the spirit of the ecumenical descend upon us. Then suddenly it came to him, his prayer answered.

"I have it," he cried, grasping the lions' heads. "I have found the way."

"To where and what, if I may ask," Bishop Kent said, yawning again.

"A way in which we may express our respective creeds yet dwell in brotherhood—on the cross."

"That cross," the Rabbi said.

The Imam shook his head.

The Archbishop leaned forward in his chair, his arms outstretched to the others.

"The crescent and the star."

"The crescent!" said the Imam.

"The star!" said the Rabbi.

The Archbishop threw himself back in the chair, lifting one leg. "Yes, we shall affix them to the cross. The cross, the crescent, and the star, the ecumenical trinity as it were."

"The star and crescent on the cross," the Archimandrite said, grasping the cross which hung from his neck.

"Well, I don't know..." the Imam said, fishing from his soutane a little pair of lemon-colored spectacles and putting them on as if to see more clearly the Archbishop's proposal.

The Rabbi said nothing, looking at the Archbishop with narrowed eyes. After all, the Jesuits had founded the Archbishop's church.

Bishop Kent coughed his dry little cough and stuck a finger

between the purple edged collar and his neck. "And what, if I may ask, would the Bishop of Rome say to such a contretemps, if I may say so?"

"The Holy Father—" the Archbishop paused. "Well, I should think…after all…what could be more ecumenical?"

No one replied and there descended the customary interval of silence, each of the divines, head down, deep in thought. When they looked up again the alarm which had been on the face of each seemed to have passed and been replaced by a kind of afflatus, as though something at last was clear.

The Rabbi was the first to speak. "My people could bring the wine, the best, from the grapes of Shiraz."

"But my dear Rabbi," the Imam said, his voice a little sharp, "as you know wine is forbidden us, spirits of any kind."

"In that case," interjected Bishop Kent, "I could bring our tent, a gay little thing we use at our annual garden party. Then the devotees of Bacchus could drink behind the flap, as it were, and thus not give offense."

"I see." The Imam folded his hands under his cloak. "Yes, a bad example would not be given."

"And I," said the Archimandrite, "could give you the use of our Katchurian cross, Archbishop, much finer than yours, rock crystal it is and tipped with silver, which means it glints in the water and so can be seen. Yours is wood and might never be found and then where would we be!"

The tambourine had begun again and the Imam commenced to tap his foot. "And I could prevail, I am sure, on the Governor General to send the band."

"I thought," said the Bishop, "that music was forbidden."

"Well," said the Imam, "just this once."

"Like the pistachio and honey cakes," said the Rabbi.

"Rabbi," the Imam winked at him, first with one eye, then with the other, "Rabbi you are tenacious, I must say. But there is one thing. It is only proper, fair, I am sure Archbishop you will agree, that if twelve of your stalwarts are to seek the cross, we must be permitted twelve of ours to seek the crescent. Isn't it so?"

"And twelve of ours to seek the star," the Rabbi said.

"And what about the maidens," added Bishop Kent. "Are they as well to come from your respective flocks?"

The Archbishop sighed. It was growing complex. Then to his surprise the Imam brushed the question of the maidens aside.

"No, no," the Imam said. "Your maidens are enough. Any youth of ours would be delighted to be garlanded by Armenian maidens. We are tolerant, you know," he giggled, "especially of Armenian maidens."

Maidens and wine, Christian, Muslim, and Jewish boys. The Archbishop felt apprehension rising in his chest. Then it finally came clear to him as, simultaneously, it did to the others.

"Ah," he said, the word dying to a despairing whisper on his lips.

"Alas," said the Rabbi.

"I fear," said Bishop Kent.

"I too," said the Archimandrite.

And the Imam, with a little pout, tilted his head in sorrow.

For they all knew. The Christian stalwarts seeking the cross, the Muslims their crescent, the Jews the star, not to mention the Greeks and the Romans, all would battle and the Katchurian would end in war, and a holy war, which was even worse.

The old men rocked back and forth, shaking their heads. In the silence the bells of the two Armenian cathedrals rang out, challenging each other. It was the angulus.

Bishop Kent stood up, brushing off the seat of his pants. "My word. It's late. I must be off to evensong."

The Imam drew his cloak around him. "And I to the mosque

for the call to prayer."

"And I am late for kaddish," the Rabbi said.

"Yes," said the Imam, standing up, "we must hurry to God."

"Don't trip on the way," the Rabbi laughed.

"Rabbi," the Imam stood on one leg, "you are too droll, always your little jokes. But," he smiled, shaking his finger at Rabbi Garbade, "we shall see, we shall see in eternity who reaches paradise first."

"Ah yes, in eternity," the Archbishop sadly said. "There at last we shall be as one. But at least," he smiled, "here in our beloved Isfahan we have come close to it, haven't we," and he thumped his staff. Then, and this time somewhat abreast, the divines made their way up the alley of willows now flooded with the light of the setting sun and into whose radiance the old men passed, a great, golden nimbus enclosing them all.

THE DUCK HUNT

THE DUCK HUNT

They looked so out of place, standing there on the quay by the sluggish, brown waters of the estuary. Their eyes so blue, the fine blond hair, the white skin and pink cheeks, something cold, clear, and shining about them, like ice in sunlight. One could imagine them sailing in the salty cold waters of the Baltic, bound for a wooded island, not here in the drowsy warmth and heaviness of the Caspian coast and bound for a place the locals called the *Morghab*, the dead lagoon.

The Osbergs were Norwegian: Count Maximilian Osberg (he used his title when abroad); his wife, Ingar; their three children, Anna, Pehr, and Lena; and the children's tutor, Johan-Erik. Every other year the Osbergs wintered in places that were hot and bright; Sicily, Greece, Spain, but this year for a change they had come to Persia, thinking the Caspian coast, in addition to the heat and light, would be an exotic, unspoiled place. They were wrong. There were villas here too and even uglier than those in Europe. And it was not so much hot as muggy. Nor, for that matter, was there much brightness, for the sky was often overcast.

Other things, too, had gone wrong. Anna, the elder daughter, 15, and Johan-Erik, the tutor, appeared to be having an affair. The Count did not approve. Affairs were permissible for men—he had had his own—but not for women, for an affair could distract a woman from her familiar duties. "But Anna is not a mother!" his wife had said with exasperation. In any event, Ingar did not disapprove of affairs for women. Then Pehr, the ten year old boy, had been unwell since they had come, nothing they could pin down, headaches, a general malaise. The Count worried—unreasonably he knew—that his own father's chronic neurasthenia had passed on to the grandson. Finally, six year old Lena had fits of quiet sobbing with no apparent cause. The Count loved Lena more than anyone.

The place the Osbergs had chosen for their sojourn was called Ghaziun—the place of the geese. They had chosen the region because it was unfashionable, unlike the resorts down the coast with their casinos, European-style hotels and royal palaces. Across the estuary from Ghaziun—a mere village—there was indeed a resort, but it was a down-at-the-heels sort of place patronized by small tradesmen, tailors, clerks, the kinds of people who could afford no more than the reed cabanas which lined the beach.

They were also the kinds of people whose ladies kept their chadors, their veils about them when wading in the sea—unlike the resorts down the coast where the ladies of the rich wore the briefest bikinis they could find. In the beginning, the Osbergs' greatest amusement was to walk the beach and watch the veiled ladies in the sea, so hilariously grotesque to see them clutching at their veils in the slap of the wind and hear their squeals when a wave swept up their legs.

"Poor creatures," Ingar would say of the veiled women, at the same time irked that she was not free to wear her own bikini. As it was, the Osbergs were stared at enough, for the people were fascinated by their whiteness and blondness and the strange color of their eyes. As time passed this staring—and sometimes laughter—had inclined the Osbergs, without their quite realizing it, to remain more and more at home.

This in part was the reason for the excursion to the *Morghab*; there would be fewer staring eyes. Also they had been told of the gigantic tulips growing in the waters of the *Morghab* and now in bloom. Finally, there was the locals' curious manner of netting ducks at night with gongs and torches. The Count was an ardent hunter—especially hunting ducks in the reedy lakes of his estate—but he had never heard of netting and wished to see it done. Because it was to be a nocturnal hunt, the Osbergs had packed a picnic supper which they planned to take at some country teahouse when night fell.

The punt the Osbergs had hired finally drew up to the quay. The boatman stood barefoot in the stern, a stocky, strong-looking young man in sky-blue pajamas—locally worn outdoors as well as in—and a sleeveless undershirt, so white against the brownness of his body. He held a punting pole in one hand while with the other he gave the Osbergs a playful, almost mocking, salute. Like all the local men, he was shaven-headed and had an oval face with eyes which made the Count think of the eyes in Byzantine icons, so black and cold, so staring they seemed unseeing and yet the Count sensed they saw everything, down to the tiny, purple birthmark that blotched his cheek.

* * *

And so the Osbergs embarked, passing out into the thick, slow waters of the estuary. To their right lay the resort, a collage of slanted tile roofs fronted by a little esplanade of neglected parterres and flaking plaster statues. To their left Ghaziun. Only the Osbergs' second story veranda—a blue bathing suit hanging on the rail—rose above the scattering of thatch cottages.

"How different everything looks from the water," the Count

said. He sat on a plank at the bow of the punt but facing the others, the children and the tutor on the next, much wider, plank, Ingar beyond, the boatman poling at the stern. The Count, a large-framed man with flowing, ginger hair, looked like the Vikings he wrote studies of—except for his shoulders which were narrow and sloped, as if in tiredness. "So different," the Count repeated.

"Of course," said Ingar, her back to him. She would have preferred the balcony and her needlework.

Soon the estuary narrowed to the width of a country road, bowered by alder and willow. Like a country road, little paths, water paths, led off of it. Down at the end of one they saw a corner of thatch roof, at the end of another, small brown horses grazing in a meadow. Some of the paths were gated with woven wattles and in one of these gated paths there was a small black boat, a crudely depicted human eye painted on the side of its high and narrow prow.

Despite these signs of human habitation, they saw not a soul, yet the place was thick with other kinds of life. Disturbed by the punt's wake, turtles plopped into the water from the banks, frogs struck out with a sudden scissor thrust and water snakes lazed alongside the punt, their elegant, swept-back heads raised above the surface of the water, surveying. The water itself, shallow, beer-colored, streamed with weed over which a haze of feeding midges hovered, and here and there the pads of some kind of water bloom floated on the water's surface. And there were birds, heron, kingfishers, others the Count could not identify, a strident chorus protesting their intrusion.

"It's oppressive," Ingar said, "like the first day of creation."

"Yes, the hot places," the Count replied, and looking up at the canopy of leaf and vine blotting out the sky and inhaling the moist, slightly scented air, he thought of his manor house, high on its tilt of land above the fjord. Trailing his hand in the weedy water, he imagined himself there now; the sappy wood crackling in the stoves, the frieze of icicles dependent from the roof, the old house stirring in the push of the wind. They would sit by the window, drinking coffee, looking at the snow.

He was brought back by the sudden lurch of the punt. The boatman had sat down on the plank at the stern and now, legs spread, was poling from side to side. The Count saw to his disgust that the boatman's pajamas were heavily pouched at the crotch, the pouch in its fullness swinging to the boatman's movement. The Count abruptly called out Ingar's name. When she turned to look at him, it was with a smile a shade too knowing, almost taunting and he thought of one of his tenant farmers who he suspected Ingar of seeing now and then and who, the local gossip claimed, was greatly endowed. There was a wildness, a carnality about Ingar which had always excited him—except when it came into play with other men and then he felt weak, unsexed, and filled with pain and anger.

Ingar turned back and the Count looked away from the obscene, swinging bag, forcing himself to think of other things, the coming duck hunt, the *Morghab's* giant tulips, the draft of his latest Viking study. Slumped against the pillowed prow, he grew drowsy in the heat and silence, only the low, rhythmic plash of the boatman's pole, hypnotic, soothing.

He was awakened by a curious sound, curious because out of context, the sucking whistle with which one calls a dog. Then to his horror he saw it was the boatman and that he was beckoning Pehr. The little boy got up and went to the boatman who eased the child down between his legs.

"Pehr!" the Count called. "Come to me!"

The child smiled back at him, shook his head, and closing his eyes, lay his head on the boatman's chest who, at the same time,

101

leaned down and briefly pressed his lips to the child's cheek.

"Ingar, Ingar!" the Count shouted. "Bring Pehr back!"

Without turning her head to him, she said: "It's nothing. They love children. I see it everywhere, on the beach, on the street, they are always embracing them, kissing them. It's their way, Max. And anyway," and now she did turn her head to him, "don't be anxious, dear," and she smiled to reassure him. "Look! How at peace Pehr seems, the calmest he's been since coming here."

"What a baby he is," Anna said, suddenly standing, her hand on Johan-Erik's head to steady herself. She was a short, tomboy-ish girl, barefoot, wearing jeans and a man's shirt. There were rings on all her fingers, given to her by some of the many town boys who, after nothing more than glimpses, wanted her.

"You are rocking the boat!" the Count said. She looked at him out of narrow eyes, shrugged, said nothing.

When the Count looked back to Pehr and the boatman, he saw that the boatman was lifting the boy up and then the boatman himself stood and pointed. They had come around a bend in the estuary and now, suddenly, there before them lay the *Morghab*, the dead lagoon.

* * *

It was not, they all agreed, what they had expected. There was its size for one thing, large as an inland sea it seemed and fur-thermore like a Sargasso Sea, so thick its waters were with weed. Then there were the numbers of small islands, black and humped which blotted its surface as far as the eye could see. As they pushed out through the weed into the lagoon, they felt on their cheeks a kind of mist or vapor and which seemed to rise from the water like an exhalation, a faintly fetid breath. The boatman shouted and again pointed and they saw in the distance a pinkish glow; it was the tulips.

By now the boatman had maneuvered the punt in amongst the pads and the children were crowding each other at the gunnels, reaching out to touch the tulips which rose up from the water on thick, hairy stalks, the blooms about a hand's breadth in size, a fleshy pink and bluntly pointed at the top. A few had opened out, petaled and floppy. Lena grabbed at one of these, breaking it from its stalk and buried her face in it depths, the petals ringing her head, a little like the wreaths the girls in Norway wore on Midsummer's Night Eve. After a moment she lifted her head, tilting it, and smiling her shy smile she said: "Oh Papa, it smells so sweet, so very sweet." The Count reached down and took her in his arms.

Meanwhile the boatman, leaning over the gunnels, was reaching out as well to the open tulips, his hand fumbling, searching at the base of the stamen for what turned out to be a black seed. When he had several of these cupped in his hand, he turned back, put one in his mouth, and smiled, licking his lips, miming their tastiness. Coming forward, he knelt before Lena, pinched a seed between his fingers, and brought it to her lips. She stared at him, not moving. Tilting his head in appeal, he began to make the same soft, sucking sound with which he had called Pehr. After a moment her lips parted, she closed her eyes, and he placed the black seed in her mouth. The other children and the tutor watching, now closed their eyes and the boatman went from one to the other, like a priest to his communicants, placing the black seeds between their parted lips. When he came to Ingar, she laughed, but she too closed her eyes, the boatman's fingers brushing her lips as he lay the seed on her outstretched tongue. Then the boatman rose from his knees and began to move toward the Count who waved him away. The Count had seen this curious practice before in the drink shops of the town where men sometimes placed pistachio nuts between each other's lips. He had been told it was an expression of some kind of fealty, in some cases perhaps of love. Whatever the meaning, its intimacy disturbed him.

Inadvertently the Count frowned at the boatman who smiled back at him. Then suddenly the boatman looked at the sky and put his hand out. A slight rain had begun to fall. The boatman went back to the gunnels and reaching out broke off some of the tulip pads. When he had several in hand, he put one on his head and indeed the pad, a good half-yard in diameter and somewhat concave in form, made an excellent rain hat. After doling out the pads—everyone laughing at the sight of each other—the boatman poled them out of the tulip pads and toward the shore and to an inlet. On the banks of the inlet stood a teahouse.

* * *

It was the usual country teahouse, a long, whitewashed building, a thatched roof extending out over its veranda. To one side of the door a long bench stood against the wall and there were several *nimkats*, bed-sized, bed-height, carpet-covered platforms. On one of these two men sat cross-legged, a water pipe and a backgammon board between them. On the ledges of the teahouse windows there were geraniums in pots.

The boatman poled them toward the little beach below the teahouse. When the punt scraped bottom, he rolled his pajamas high on his thighs and jumped into the water. Half pushing and half rocking the punt, he brought the Osbergs close enough to the little beach so that they might jump ashore. After Ingar had seen to Lena and Pehr, she turned back to look at the boatman striding up out of the water, his thighs gleaming in their wetness.

"What beautiful legs," Ingar said, turning to the Count who looked away from the swinging bag.

A young man followed by an old woman came out the teahouse door, both hailing the boatman whom it was apparent they knew. The boatman bowed to the old woman, shook the young man's hand and there followed the usual, lengthy formal expressions of esteem and deference which a Persian greeting entails. Next, and speaking in the local dialect, the boatman, motioning with his head toward the Osbergs, explained who they were and what they were about. The teahouse keeper smiled, bowing to the Osbergs, while the old woman came forward and put her hand on Lena's head, alternately smiling at Ingar and raising her eyes to the sky and Ingar understood—this precious gift from God.

The ceremony of greeting completed, all was activity. The boatman and the teahouse keeper pushed two of the *nimkats* together to make a platform capacious enough for all the Osbergs to lounge upon. The old woman brought out long, sausage-shaped bolsters and a white table cloth which she lay at the center of the *nimkats*. Meanwhile the teahouse keeper reappeared with a tray of tea in little fluted glasses painted with tiny blue flowers—forget-me-nots, Ingar thought.

The Osbergs drank their tea and looked about, smiling. The teahouse, the beach, the little inlet, all these created an opening in the dense and tangled woodland, air and space and sky, headroom as it were. At the same time the *Morghab*—so somber with its humped, black islands—was cut off from their view by the inlet's bend.

"It's so peaceful…at last," Ingar said. "So safe, it seems. I wonder…" With both hands she swept her hair back from her face.

People in Norway said she had the face of a ship's figurehead, thrust forward and staring and with its rounded, waxen beauty.

No one answered her. The only sound in the silence was the clatter now and then of the backgammon counters and a murmuring from the teahouse into which the boatman, the teahouse keeper, and the old woman had retired. Nothing happened. It was one of those occasions when people say that time has stopped.

"We are like a pool," the Count remarked to himself, "a still pool reflecting the sky, the trees beyond, that bench against the wall. I am content." And saying so he realized it was the first time on this strange coast that he had felt at peace. And Ingar, too, had just expressed the same.

So deep was he in his reverie that he saw with surprise the teahouse keeper standing before him. The man was gesturing, his hand going back and forth to his mouth, then putting his hands together he tilted his head to rest it on them. It was clear; did they wish to eat or sleep? The Count turned to Ingar. "A nap before supper?" She nodded. The Count turned back to the teahouse keeper and closed his eyes. The man bowed and went away.

The Count lay back on his side, curled up, his head cradled in the crook of his arm. He was ready for sleep, sinking down into it despite the flies which flicked his hands and face. But he soon awoke to feel something covering him. It was cloth. Pushing it aside, he saw that it was a chador. Someone had put it over him to protect him from the flies he supposed and he pulled it back again. It smelled of woman's hair, faintly of perfume, and of dust. The perfume, the smell of the hair, the chador itself reminded him of one of the bathing women who had looked at him and he at her and something he had no name for had passed between them. He wanted to push the chador aside again but in the end he gave in to it, succumbed to it and in its folds he slept.

The others did not sleep. Ingar lay on her back staring at the sky. Pehr and the teahouse keeper squatted on the banks of the inlet, the teahouse keeper with his knife making little boats of bark for Pehr to float. Lena, in the teahouse, lay cradled in the arms of the old woman who, rocking her, sang in a husky, cracked voice a local lullaby. Anna and Johan-Erik had wandered off into the woods seeking a sequestered place. When they found it, Anna stood against a tree, Johan-Erik against her and they copulated fiercely. The boatman watched from behind a mound of rock, smiling, his hand in the pouch, caressing.

"Ingar, Ingar," the Count called out in his sleep.

She rolled over to him, put her hand on his brow, and whispered in his ear: "I am here, I am here, don't fret, my dear." He woke up. "You were dreaming?" He looked away, saying nothing. "Come. Dusk is here. It's time for supper. Pehr, Lena," she called. "Where is Anna?"

They unpacked the supper; fish cakes, rice, hard boiled eggs, the local flat bread, some fruit and beer.

"Anna," Ingar called again. "Johan-Erik."

They answered, coming out from the forest. The Count looked at them and knew.

"But where is Lena?" Ingar asked with irritation and called again. Then she saw Lena standing in the teahouse door, a kitten in her arms. Burying her face in the squirming kitten's neck, she came down to them. "We have a guest," she said with her shy smile and put the kitten down on the *nimkat*, the kitten wobbling off in the direction of the food.

"*No!*" shouted Ingar, picking the kitten up and throwing it to the ground. Lena's face went white, still, staring wide-eyed at her mother. No one spoke. Then the storm broke, Lena's face twisting into hurt and anger and from her throat came what sounded like a long hiccup and then the sobs began, her whole body shaking in their force. The old woman ran down from the terrace, swept Lena up into her arms, and, rocking the child, began to coo to her.

"*No, no, no,*" said Ingar, almost yelling. "No, we don't do that. It's not our way. We let her cry. She must learn," forgetting in her agitation that the old woman understood nothing of what she said. By now the teahouse keeper was at the old woman's side and touching her shoulder, he shook his head. Finally she let him take the child which he carried to Ingar who set Lena down with a hard thump at her side. The sobs rose to a scream which tore the silence of the place. The old woman grabbed at the Koranic amulet hanging from her neck and, whispering a prayer, pressed it to her heart.

* * *

By the time they had finished supper, night had fallen and the boatman signaled that they should start for the hunt. The teahouse keeper brought lanterns to light their way to the banks of the inlet. There they found a second punt, two old men with punt poles standing in its stern. This punt was somewhat larger than their own and its prow hooded with a black tarp. Beneath the hood a flare burned in a little bowl, its flicker throwing shadows which leaped and twisted in its light. Lena took her father's hand. Was it the shadows, the Count wondered, or had she remembered the cobra they had seen the summer before at the Homburg zoo, coweled as was this punt and to which the boatman now beckoned them?

Once aboard, the teahouse keeper made them understand that he would be in the other punt playing the gong and he showed it to them, slipping it out of a blue velvet case, a saucer-sized disk of brass hanging from a rod and engraved with Arabic script. The teahouse keeper mimed prayer and then pointed to the disk's inscriptions. He showed them, too, the gong stick, padded at its end with a ball of cloth. When he struck the gong with it, it seemed to the Count as though the gong paused before releasing its clang, then moving out in circles of sound, ever widening, ever fainter, and the Count thought of his earlier reverie of content and now it was as if a stone had been dropped into the pool of the night. He shook his head and held Lena's hand more tightly to bring him back to what the boatman was showing them; it was the net.

It consisted of a handle about the diameter and length of a long broom stick, at its end and somewhat longer than the handle, an elliptical shaped net, its mouth rimmed and held open by willow sticks. At its bottom the net was doubled to form a little pocket—the trap.

By now one of the old men and the teahouse keeper had removed to the other punt, the old man standing in the stern with his pole, the teahouse keeper squatting in front of him, holding high the gong which glinted now and then as it swung from its rod in the punt's drift. In the hooded punt the boatman, after rocking the punt free of the shallow water, had taken up his position behind the hood, the net upright in his hand. They were ready to move out, and signaling this, the gong began to sound.

The punts, one behind the other, took on surprising speed as they passed from the inlet into a narrow waterway bordered on either side by willows and banks of reed. As they went on the vegetation became heavier, the overhanging willows now low above the punt. The shadows cast by the flare thrashed around them, the gong clanging a kind of wild accompaniment.

"Max!" Ingar called out in a voice that was like a cry.

"Madame," the boatman whispered and put his finger to his lips.

The Count leaned forward and as he did so he heard a splash. Looking in the direction of the sound, he saw a mallard rise from the reeds, flash in the light of the flare, the beating of its wings near and loud above the clanging of the gong.

A little farther on the boatman pointed and they saw two mallards beneath an over-hanging willow. The boatman began his sucking whistle and the gong stopped, the rings of sound fading into silence. This time when the mallards rose into the air, the net came swooping down, netting the drake. The boatman came forward to show it to the others, a bulge of feathers, pulsing in the pocket at the bottom of the net. For a moment he cupped the pocket in his hand and then swung the net to Pehr who cupped the pocket, too, and from Pehr the net swung on to the other children, to Johan-Erik, to Ingar, each in turn cupping their hands around the throbbing sack of life, feeling the blood rush of the creature. As the net approached the Count, he reared back but it found him, grazing his face, and its burden softly touched his lips. With a loud, hoarse gasp, he fell against the cushions in the bow, his face contorted in the flare-light.

"Max!" Ingar called, scrambling across the children to reach him. She shook him by his shoulders and looked into his staring eyes. "Max!" she called again. "It's alright! We'll go back, back." She turned to the boatman who had removed the drake from the net to lock its wings. "Go back, go back," she said in Norwegian, then in English, forgetting in her panic that he understood neither.

"Ghaziun," Anna yelled at him. Smiling, he dipped his head to her. Spreading his legs and leaning back a little to steady

himself, and with one strong thrust of his pole, he turned the
punt around, laughing.

* * *

The Osbergs cut short their stay on the Caspian coast. The following winter they remained in their old manor house, high
on its tilt of land above the fjord. Sometimes sitting by the
window, drinking their coffee, watching the snow slanting
down into the fjord below, they would talk of their stay in
Ghaziun; of the veiled women bathing in the sea, the dead
lagoon and its giant tulips, the teahouse and the duck hunt.

"But sometimes I wish that we had never gone," Ingar said
one afternoon. The Count did not reply but turned from the
window and looked at her. Ingar stood up then and went to
him and standing put her hand on the slope of his shoulder.
For a little while they were silent, watching the snow slant
down, down into the fjord.

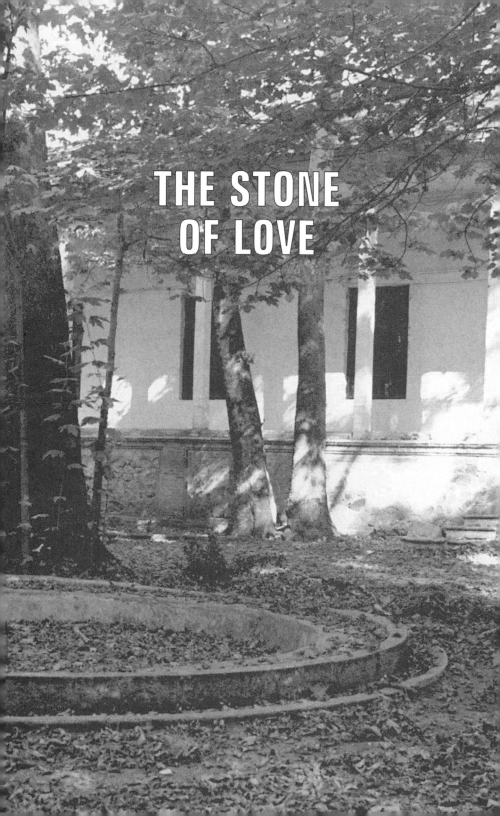

THE STONE
OF LOVE

THE STONE OF LOVE

It was my custom for some years to leave my farm each summer and go for a month of holiday to a small resort on the Caspian coast of Persia called Bandar Pahlavi. One of the things I liked about the place was its hotel. Built at the turn of the century, it was a gray, rather classical building with potted orange trees by the door and long, pedimented windows which looked down on the quay and across the estuary to the swaged tile rooftops of the town. In general it was a most comfortable old place. The rooms were high-ceilinged and cool, each with a broad writing table drawn up before its window. Also there was a tower, glassed in at the top, where guests might sit on moonlit nights and look out at the sea.

For me, however, the main attraction of the hotel was its courtyard. This was a flagstoned area surrounded by white, long-windowed walls and overhung on all sides by wide roof-eaves from which swung down long strands of vine. In the center of the courtyard stood a substantial arbor supported on columns into which at intervals little masks—like gargoyles, grimacing and taunting—had been carved. This arbor, and the long table under it, served as a modest buffet; cold ham and sturgeon, baskets of fruit, the good local black bread and jam. Also candles burned on the arbor table, alone among the tables in the courtyard.

Repairing to the courtyard in the evening was the climax of

my day, one which I dearly enjoyed and looked forward to from morning. After bathing and putting on fresh clothes, I would go down at dusk to my table in the corner and there begin the evening's peace; a carafe of vodka, my journal, a book, the other guests to speculate upon, the candles burning in the arbor's leafy gloom.

It was here one evening that the experience occurred which this story is about. I don't know how to name what happened. Perhaps it might best be called a waking dream. It would not be accurate to call it a vision. I am an ordinary man and do not have them. And anyway in a vision, I believe, one sees some kind of truth. That did not happen here for in the end the truth was not given.

Before relating what happened, I should mention two things. The first is that I had never heard nor read about the persons and events which were present in the dream. Concerning only one thing did I have prior knowledge: before the time of air-travel, Bandar Pahlavi had been the port from which most Persians set out for the West, traveling to Baku by ship and from there by train to Europe.

The second point is this. I do not believe in the supernatural. I have never seen a ghost. On the other hand, since childhood I have in certain places felt the past and its people around me—not tangibly but present nonetheless, present in the empty air.

Beyond this I can give no further explanation of what took place.

The evening on which the dream occurred was like any other evening. I had, as usual, sat down at the corner table and as usual Hossein, the old waiter, had brought my carafe of vodka. Nearby there was a table of merchants out for a little spree, gorging on caviar and wine. Farther down the courtyard sat a group of young Persian women wearing bright, summer dresses, seemingly the guests of a much older woman, a tall, bowed figure who, in the then old Persian manner, was entirely veiled in black.

Having enjoyed for a time the gusto of the merchants, and imagined some conversation for the ladies and their old and honored hostess, I turned to begin my vodka and it was then, as I raised my glass while at the same time glancing at the burning lights within the arbor, that the strange dream began and my mind became a screen and I saw projected on it the travelers and their story.

All, it seemed, had traveled in private coaches from Tehran to Rasht, a town twelve miles inland from Bandar Pahlavi. There they had boarded separate launches and sailed in a little flotilla down the estuary, arriving at the hotel quay at dusk. After registering for the night—for all were embarking the next morning on the Russian steamer for Baku—they retired to their respective rooms to dine.

The travelers were as follows. His Excellency, Moin al-Molk, Persian Ambassador to Vienna, en route to Vienna. Next, His Grace, Alexis Manisian, Archimandrite of the Persian Armenians of the Gregorian Rite, en route to Yerevan in Russian Armenia, the seat of his church. Then Teymour Khan Bakhtiar, youngest son of Mohammad Ali Khan, Persian Minister of War, en route with his tutor, Mirza Hossein, to Geneva where Teymour Khan was to be enrolled in a school for young noblemen. Next, Madame Maria Petanoff, en route to her native Kiev and to retirement after some years as mistress to Motamed Doleh, the Shah's uncle. Finally, Nasser Goharian, a jewel merchant, en route to various places.

It was a close evening, as is often the case on the Caspian coast, and for this reason several of the travelers came down to the courtyard to take their tea and smoke; the Ambassador, Teymour Khan and his tutor, Mirza Hossein, and the jewel merchant. The other travelers were also present though at a little distance. On one side of the courtyard there was a large, bow-shaped balcony and here, as though on a throne, sat the Archimandrite, reading his breviary, fanned by a servant. Three windows away sat Madame Petanoff, looking out.

In the courtyard the men became acquainted. Mirza Hossein, the tutor, presented Teymour Khan to the Ambassador. The jewel merchant presented himself. Teymour Khan and the Ambassador exchanged the usual, interminable Persian courtesies and then the Ambassador, growing bored, invited Mirza Hossein to a game of backgammon and the board was brought. Meanwhile Teymour Khan and the jewel merchant settled down at the table under the arbor and began to talk of Europe and particularly about the customs of Europe and how they differed from those of Persia.

"My father tells me," Teymour Khan said, "that the young men of Europe do not wear jewels." And he spread out his hands. On the long fingers with their pointed nails there were a good dozen rings set with fine but gaudy gems. He smiled. "I shall set a new fashion," and he raised and turned his hand before his face.

"Perhaps," said Nasser Goharian.

"Not perhaps," said Teymour, angered by the impertinence. The jeweler was of no rank, and worse, had no idea of how to behave toward rank.

And in fact Nasser, alone among the travelers, was not a person of rank nor was there in his appearance anything of natural distinction. He was a short, fat man with tufts of hair in his ears and a perpetual, silly grin on his round face. Only the Ambassador had noticed that he moved his hands with a mesmerizing grace.

Sorry that he had offended Teymour and hoping to smooth his feelings, Nasser said: "Your rings are very precious and indeed beautiful, Teymour Khan."

"You are a judge?"

"To some extent. I am sorry—perhaps I neglected to say when I presented myself. I am a jewel merchant. That in fact is the purpose of my journey. I am taking a number of my gems abroad. I wonder," he raised his head and pitched his voice higher, "would you, I wonder, care to see the jewels?" The click of the backgammon counters stopped. Madame Petanoff at her window leaned slightly out. Even the Archimandrite, murmuring his breviary, paused and looked down.

"Why indeed, Goharian," spoke up the Ambassador. "You are most kind. How pleasantly it will pass our evening." Then he stood and addressed the Archimandrite on the balcony. "Your Grace, do join us," and then turning to Madame Petanoff he bowed. "And you, Madame. We should be most honored if you would grace our party." The Archimandrite and Madame Petanoff smiled and bowed forward in their chairs.

"Nasser Goharian," said the Ambassador, "would you be so kind as to order ice and lime water—and lamps too, I think, for it is growing dark. We can view the jewels here at the arbor table if that is agreeable with you."

"Of course, Excellency," said Nasser, and all the travelers in the courtyard sat down around the table. Soon the Archimandrite joined them, a tall old man with ice blue eyes and a great bib of white beard. Madame Petanoff followed shortly, dressed in black with a silk rose at her breast, still a splendid looking woman with her milk-white skin, shining eyes, and great, high bun of gleaming auburn hair, a woman at the very pitch of ripeness.

After Madame Petanoff had seated herself and introductions

were made all around, the servant brought the lime water and the lamps and the travelers began to drink and to chat about their coming journey. These formalities observed, the Ambassador turned to Nasser Goharian and said: "Well, Nasser Goharian, what about these gems of yours. Shall we be privileged to see them?"

"Of course, Excellency. I was only waiting for your command." And Nasser took the jewel case from inside his coat, a rectangular board with an inlay of purple felt and a narrow drawer in either end. The light of the lamps lay bright on the case and on the hands of the travelers, resting open or clenched or splayed out on the tabletop.

Nasser pulled out the little drawers and began, one by one, to place the gems on the purple felt. The travelers leaned forward, looking closely at the spangle of jewels: dark, pigeon-blood rubies; an oval emerald; a pair of matched sapphires; a milk-blue moonstone. The board blazed and crackled like fire under the lamplight.

"Superb," said Madame Petanoff, softly. The Ambassador nodded, saying nothing. Mirza Hossein's eyes went from stone to stone, searching. The Archimandrite, after a time, looked away. The ringed right hand of Teymour Khan stretched toward the board.

"But these, my friends, are nothing," said Nasser. "Here is the treasure, the true treasure of all, of everything." And he took from his pocket a chamois pouch. He weighed it for a moment in his hand and then opened it. A small ebony apple rolled on to the board. He let it lay for a moment and then took it again in his hands and cupped it there. When he opened his hands, the apple was quartered to its base and there on a bud of black silk lay a diamond, its brilliance blinding the travelers like acetylene.

"It is quite priceless," Nasser said. For once the silly grin had left his face and he looked down at the gem with sorrow. "Priceless," he said again. Then he straightened up and smiled. "But not for the reason you think. There are many diamonds in the world as large as this, a fair number much larger. No, it is priceless because, you see, it is flawed, flawed perfectly." And he laughed. "Look," he continued, and he pushed the board farther into the middle of the table. "Look into its center." The travelers leaned forward and looking into the diamond they saw at its heart a black star.

There was a long silence and on the face of each of the travelers there appeared a still, abstracted look as if the rays of the blazing star had pierced through to some deep focus of memory and desire in each. Then the apple in the cup of Nasser's hand clicked shut and the travelers came to life again, all speaking at once and moving about in their chairs, again as they had been before seeing the black star at the diamond's heart.

The Ambassador was the first to address Nasser. "Yes, indeed a most remarkable gem. As you say, Nasser, quite priceless. But of course when we say an object is priceless, we simply mean that its price is very high. At what do you value this gem?"

"I have never estimated its value, Excellency, and for the simple reason that it is not for sale. It cannot be sold."

The travelers smiled. It was an old ruse of merchants when they had in their possession something rare and beautiful.

"Come, come," said the Ambassador. "We are not dealing now my good Nasser. This is only a matter of curiosity. Let us say that it had caught the eye of His Majesty, about what would the price be?"

"If His Majesty could open the apple, Excellency, he might have the diamond for nothing. Yes, anyone who opens the apple may have the gem. You are most welcome to try though, if you will forgive me, I doubt that you will succeed. But if you wish…" and Nasser passed the ebony apple to the Ambassador.

The apple went from hand to hand. The Ambassador felt for hidden springs. Teymour Khan wrenched at its top. Mirza Hossein had it tightly in his hands and murmured a spell. The Archimandrite with his forefinger drew a cross on its side. Madame Petanoff raised it to her lips.

By now it had grown late and the lamps had burned low. Nasser returned the apple to its pouch and the jewels to their drawers. Then rising and asking the permission of the company to depart, he bade them all good night and retired to his room. There he put the case and pouch under his pillow, lay down, and fell into a deep and dreamless sleep. The sleep of the others was neither deep nor dreamless for the diamond and its black star burned in their minds like a holy fire.

The following morning Nasser was called upon by each of the travelers. The Ambassador was first.

"Nasser Goharian," said the Ambassador, "let us get down to business. I want the diamond and I am prepared to pay a good price—though mind you, a fair one." The Ambassador stated a sum and took out his purse.

"Excellency," said Nasser, throwing out his hands, "believe me. I would not trifle with you. Last night was no merchant's dodge. I cannot sell the diamond to you."

The Ambassador rose and walked to the window, his back to Nasser. Then he turned and said: "I cannot offer you more than I already have for the gem. But I can do this. As you might imagine, I have much influence at court. In the past His Majesty has been most generous in granting my small requests. Now; as you may or may not know, there is at present no Court Jeweler—old Ramazan died several months ago. I am ready to propose you for the post. As you well know, Nasser, the Court is a place of great power. Any man in your position would give anything for what I offer you." The Ambassador paused. "Now, Nasser, I think you must be satisfied. Here is the money and my promise. Give me the jewel."

Nasser said nothing, his eyes down. Finally, he raised his head. "My dear Excellency, please forgive me. It simply cannot be done." The Ambassador flushed. Nasser, hoping to cool his anger, said: "Tell me, dear Excellency, why do you want the jewel so much? What does it mean to you?"

The Ambassador sat down and looked carefully at Nasser as if to determine whether his question had been an idle one. What he saw—perhaps the sadness beneath the silly grin—must have reassured him. "Some years ago, Nasser Goharian, when I was a young attaché in Paris, I had an affair with a woman who—well, it is not material. At any rate, there was a child, a girl. The mother died. The child is now sixteen." The Ambassador stopped. He took from a pocket a small, oval case, and from his waistcoat pocket a gold nail. "This picture," he said, opening the case, "goes with me everywhere. It hangs on this nail above my head wherever I sleep. This beauty..." he softly said. "Nasser Goharian, never, never in my life have I loved as I have loved this child. For her I would do anything. I would desecrate the shrines of our holy Imams, anything. And so out of my love all these years I have been searching for some perfect purity, some perfect beauty to give to her, something that would encase, contain my love. And now I have found it. Nasser Goharian, you must give me the jewel!"

Nasser laid his hand on the Ambassador's arm. "Your story has touched me, Excellency, your love. But..." and his hand fell, "I cannot give you the stone nor tell you the secret of the apple."

The Ambassador rose and walked to the door. Without turning, he said, "You are a fool, Nasser. The appointment at Court means power...power!"

"But Excellency," said Nasser, "power is not the way."

Madame Petanoff was the next to call, accompanied by her maid. After a nod from her mistress, the maid withdrew to the far end of the room and sat down by a window. Then Madame Petanoff began in a low voice to speak to Nasser. "Nasser Goharian, I have come to see you about your wares. Some of the pieces which you showed us last evening were charming but, of course, and as you yourself said, the diamond is the treasure. In fact it is the diamond," she paused, "the diamond which I have come about. I hope you will be reasonable, not hard on me." She smiled. The smile was part of her beauty. It had gained her much. "What, Nasser, do you want for it?"

"Madame Petanoff," Nasser said, "I wish I were simply free to give you the gem. That is my wish. But believe me, I am not free to either give or sell."

Madame Petanoff glanced down the room to her maid, and then quietly moved her chair closer to Nasser. "Nasser Goharian, for certain reasons the jewel means everything to me. So much, so much, you cannot know. Besides the money," she paused, "besides the money—and I can give you a good price—besides that..." she stopped again. And then gathering herself and looking at him, she said: "After all we are to be fellow travelers as far as Kiev. We may be..." she looked away, "we may be companions, Nasser Goharian." She quickly glanced at him, and then away again.

Nasser stood up and touched her lightly on the shoulder. "Indeed the jewel must mean much to you," he said.

Madame Petanoff said nothing for a moment and then beckoned to her maid. "Tasha, go to the room and begin the packing." When the girl had left, she walked down the room and took the maid's place at the window. "You know, of course, who I am, of my connection with Motamed Doleh.

What you do not know, what few know, is that this connection was not of the usual kind. I loved him. And now…" and she let her head fall onto her folded arms. After a moment she raised her head and began again. "When this, this separation occurred, my love, so great, became as great a hate. I sold everything, every jewel he had ever given me. I despised them and I wanted their place taken by something base, anonymous, by money. But now," she turned back from the window and looked again at Nasser, "but now my heart is broken with regret. Now, again, I want some reminder of our love, something, some one thing that I may keep. So I would use the money from those jewels and with it take your diamond and then once again I would have something from him, a token of his once great love. My beauty will soon pass, Nasser. Let me take the diamond to remind me of it and of our love. Give me the diamond, Nasser."

"Your story, Madame Petanoff," Nasser said, "has touched me greatly. Of course, I see now why the jewel means everything to you. And so it grieves me to say again…" Madame Petanoff rose from her chair and slowly walked up the room to stop when she was very close to him.

"Nasser," she said, "this beauty. Look at it, this beauty…yours."

"No," he said. "Beauty is not the way."

Teymour Khan, the next to call, barely knocked before entering and he began his business at once. "Nasser Goharian, I want the diamond. And let us have no nonsense about the price. After all, it is flawed."

"And so not suitable for Your Excellency," said Nasser.

"I am the one to decide that, jeweler," replied Teymour Khan. "Don't worry; I shall give you a decent price." The Khan took a roll of bills from his pocket and laid them on the table. "Now the diamond. I must pack yet, I am late. Please give me the diamond immediately."

"Teymour Khan, I regret that I must repeat what I said last night. The gem is not for sale." Nasser stood up. "And now I believe we are both late with our packing."

Teymour Khan leaned back in his chair, smiling, his chin resting on his fisted hand. "Nasser Goharian," he said, pointing to the bills on the table, "that is a great deal of money. But if it is not enough, I have something else to give you which may change your mind. You know, Nasser, who my father is. You perhaps know too of his—how shall I say—of his famous temper. I am his favorite son. He would not want me thwarted."

"And why," Nasser sighed, "do you, Teymour Khan, want the stone?"

"Because," said Teymour, "it matches me. It no doubt shocks you, no matter; you see I love myself and very much. I have seen no one finer than myself. And now in the world of things I have found the finest, my match, my twin, and I shall have it." Teymour Khan stood up. "Come! I've no time to waste. Take the money and give me the stone."

Nasser Goharian turned away from Khan. "I must repeat, Excellency, the gem is not for sale."

Teymour Khan stepped suddenly, swiftly forward, his hand raised. "Beware, Nasser Goharian, beware!"

"No, no Excellency," said Nasser. "Fear is never the way."

The next to come to Nasser was Mirza Hossein, the tutor. He stooped in the doorway, ingratiating. Nasser gently asked him in. After much circling, Mirza Hossein came at last to the matter of the diamond. Like the others, he offered a sum of money and, like the others, when this was refused, he made a second proposal.

"I have in my possession, Nasser Goharian, a most remarkable manuscript. It is a compendium—a unique one, there is no copy—of the magical properties of jewels. Like your diamond, it has never been for sale, I have never dreamt of such a thing. But now, Nasser, I am ready, together with the money, to give it in exchange for the diamond." The old man sat forward, his hands on his knees, his eyes pleading.

"I understand, Mirza Hossein, said Nasser, "that in making this offer you make a great sacrifice, that this manuscript means much to you. And so you must forgive me—no, I cannot give the diamond in exchange for anything."

Mirza Hossein slowly stood up, his eyes casting desperately around the room. "I must have the diamond, I must. Let me tell you and perhaps then you will have mercy." He walked away from Nasser and stood facing the wall, his hands trembling a little, clasped behind his back. "Soon Teymour Khan is to leave me. There will be nothing left. I will come back to Persia and die and the greatest wish of my life, the truest love, the strongest desire of this awful life will go ungranted." The old man turned from the wall to face Nasser. "Last night I pretended to sleep. After a little while, I saw Teymour Khan rise from his bed and stand there naked before the pier glass, rubbing his loins and breast with perfumed oils. Then he slipped out the door and down the hall to lie with the Russian whore. With the diamond, Nasser, if it were mine to give, he would come to me. Then, at last, this passion would be at rest and I might die in peace." His hands up, as though to ward off a blow, the old man walked slowly toward the jeweler. "Have pity," he said, "oh, Nasser Goharian, have pity!"

"No," said Nasser gently, "nor is pity the way."

The last to come to Nasser was Alexis, the Archimandrite. He took the seat by the window and Nasser brought a chair to join him. They chatted casually like old friends for a little while. Then Alexis, gathering his skirts and folding his hands in his lap, began. "You know, of course, why I have come, Nasser Goharian. I suppose the others have come as well. All were bewitched by the jewel—as am I."

"Yes," said Nasser, "they all want it, but none know the way."

"The way, no doubt, my good Nasser, is a king's ransom," said Alexis, laughing.

"No," replied Nasser.

"Ah, that I am happy to hear," said Alexis, "for I have no such sum to offer you, only a modest amount plus my prayers and something infinitely precious which no money can match, for I want the gem to adorn one of those tributes which we construct in church and mosque to honor Him, to show our love. Here, I shall tell you." Alexis settled back in his chair, the tips of his slippers pointing up from under his skirts, his hand on his pectoral cross. "When I was a boy, before going off to seminary, I apprenticed myself to my uncle, a goldsmith. There, though I never became a master craftsman, I learned the rudiments of the craft. Later, after receiving my vocation and leaving for the seminary, I promised in my gratitude to God that I would devote the free hours of my life to working with all my skill a cross of gold which I would place when finished on the alter of St. Gregory, the place where kneeling as a boy in our Cathedral at Yerevan I received my vocation. Now, Nasser, the cross is almost finished. I have worked at it these 40 years, engraving and working the gold, setting it with precious stones. Only one part of the cross have I left unfinished, the place where, were it a crucifix, my Savior's head would rest. This I have not dared to touch. This, I believed, should be left free of human effort, presumption. Yes, this I thought until last night when I saw the diamond with its perfect flaw...that stone of love."

Nasser Goharian looked into the Archimandrite's eyes and then he bowed and shook his head.

128

"Oh, Nasser," said Alexis, "in God's name I ask you, give the stone, give it for the love of God."

Nasser turned and looked out the window, down the slope of land and to the sea and sky beyond. "Even the love of God is not the way," he said.

And as he said it, the bell of the little steamer clanged, signaling that it was time for the travelers to embark—and I woke up, as it were, aware again of the courtyard around me, of the merchants and the Persian ladies, and of Hossein, the waiter, running toward my table. For a heavy wind had suddenly swept down on us and it had overturned my vodka glass. The courtyard was like the bottom of a vortex, the long strands of vine swinging wildly in the wind, bits of refuse flying through the air. Hossein picked up my glass and told me to go in, that rain would shortly come, and as he spoke it started, pelting down in big summer drops. I motioned him away, for I desired with all my will to return to the dream, to learn its ending, for surely it had been cut short. And so I sat on in the rain, my eyes searching inward to find again the travelers. But nothing came. However much I tried, the screen remained a blank. Finally, looking up, I saw that the lights within the arbor had blown out and I got up and went.

In my room I immediately went to bed, hoping that I might return to the dream in true sleep, and I did dream, but only of an empty sea. The next day instead of chatting with the beach vendors and the children as I usually did, I kept to my bathing cabin and there I tried, again and again, to enter the dream, remembering in sequence its every detail. But I was always brought up short, never able to go beyond the clanging of the bell.

A week later it was the end of summer and I left Bandar Pahlavi to return to my farm. There, often through that winter

I would try, sitting by the fire, to imagine the dream's ending. For after all the travelers had not finished their journey, had only just begun it, and surely they, who wanted the stone so much, surely one of them would find the way, and then I would know it too.

In time I gave up trying to find the answer from the travelers and began to tell the story of the dream to other people, hoping that I would find someone who might know its ending. I first told my servant, a boy of some intelligence with a simple, folk mind, hoping that with his mother wit he could tell me the sequel of my dream. I seemed only to puzzle him. Next I tried the few people who now and then turn up here at the farm; they too had no answer. Once on a journey back to my native West, I questioned those people I ran across whom I thought might know—my confessor in Milan, a woman in Marseilles who, whore to many sea-captains, had heard many strange tales, a learned old rabbi in Leipzig, my father, my friend, the wise and the foolish, the depraved and the good. But no one knew.

As time passes, I wish more and more that I had never had the dream for it nags so at my soul, and more and more I fear that I shall never learn its ending or find someone who does, and that finally for me, as for the other travelers, the stone of love with its perfect flaw will lie forever locked away in the blackness of the apple.

MRS. CAHN

MRS. CAHN

The van sped down the narrow, steep, and rocky road. The driver looked at his companion as often as he looked at the road and never did he glance to his left and the deep ravines which fell away from the road without benefit of guard rails. Sometimes he would take both hands off the wheel to sketch pictures in the air to illustrate his tale. Both driver and companion were much given to laughter and sometimes to a joshing punch in the ribs. Behind them in the van sat eleven terrified Americans.

The van and its passengers had started out in the morning from the Persian city of Shiraz. The Americans, on an archaeological tour of Persia's ancient monuments and ruins, were on their way to the valley of Shahpur and a cave there which contained a mammoth statute of Shahpur I, a fourth century Persian king.

Originally the tour was to have been limited to the board members of a small but famous American museum of Middle Eastern art and artifact. In the end only three of the board members signed up. The remainder of the group, nine in all, had little interest in the Middle East and not much more in archaeology. Rather they were the kinds of people who went on tours for the companionship they offered; people who wanted someone else, a tour director, for example, to make decisions for them; people who were beginning to run out of exotic destinations that were both safe and comfortable. Finally there were those who joined because they had been told by the travel agent, the instigator of the tour, that the group would consist mainly of the rich and socially prominent board members of the famous museum.

The board members who had joined the tour were two scholars and an old woman named Mrs. Cahn. The scholars, ostensibly "resource persons" for the archaeological sites, kept to themselves, shared a room at the various hotels and, it was whispered, shared a bed as well. The old woman, Mrs. Cahn, had joined the tour to educate herself. She was from a family who had long been benefactors of the arts and other worthy causes. It was a family rule, however, that any family member giving to such institutions must keep abreast of that institution's activities. Since Mrs. Cahn had only recently joined the board of the museum, she believed it her duty to inform herself and join the tour.

"Imperious" was the term often used to describe Mrs. Cahn. She was a very tall old woman and through an almost constant effort of will she was absolutely erect as well. Her height was emphasized by a high crown of marcelled white hair from which—at least on dressy occasions—she let a curl fall, like Josephine, Napoleon's consort, and a woman she much admired. Then there was Mrs. Cahn's face, especially the nose and eyes, a great prow of a nose, nobly arched, the nostrils flared, the eyes large, black, brimming with light—though some said with a hint of rancor in them. All this combined with a pronouncedly lifted chin. It was a magnificent head and in a curious way accented by its perpetual nodding, for Mrs. Cahn suffered from a tremor of the head.

During the day Mrs. Cahn dressed rather like a nineteenth century Quaker lady or a nun, long, gray skirts, a shirtwaist of the same gray color, an almost clerical white collar. On sunny days she topped her elaborate coiffure with a wide-brimmed straw hat. At night Mrs. Cahn wore her jewels, a fair number of them, and a famous couturier's "basic black."

Mrs. Cahn did not care for her fellow tour members, especially the scholars. Though she liked men very much—far more than women—prissy men did not appeal to her. As for the others, she judged them vulgar and so dismissed them from her attention.

The Persians she had met fared no better. Vulgar too. The Embassy had arranged—pressured, she suspected—the governor-general of the province to entertain the tour to dinner. They trooped off to an exquisite little eighteenth century palace and into a hideous room filled with pseudo-Louis XIV gilt, a dense canopy of dusty chandeliers and at each of their places a bottle of Pepsi Cola and a Kleenex for a napkin. The governor-general she had found a repellent little man, an obvious time-server. She could spot a time-server easily, having known so many at home. Then there were the waiters in their hotel; difficult to tell whether they were smiling or sneering. Spoiled by tourists, she supposed. And finally their interpreter, the most energetic sycophant she had ever encountered (and she had encountered many because of her great wealth), this one always fishing for an invitation to "your great country."

Yes, vulgar, both her own people and the Persians. It was a word she found herself using more and more frequently these days and that worried her, that and her increasing irritability. Perhaps it was simply that she was old, unwell, and tired. Tired of forcing herself to stand erect, tired of fools, tired of her vast fortune, now a burden rather than a pleasure. And no one needed her, her sons in New York obsessed with making millions they did not need and the fretful and spoiled grandchildren whom she really did not care for as much as she knew she should. In general, and in her own phrasing of it, she felt used up, finished, that there was really nothing more for her to do except to die. Yes, with death it would all be over, the tedium, the pain, the uselessness, everything. She turned and looked out the van window, down into the ravines, green in their depths, distant, empty with peace. Idly she wondered, laughing to herself, whether if they went over the edge, she would descend headfirst or feet first and then remembered she would be captive in the van. But at least she would look out the window and catch a glimpse of the ravine's rock wall, better than staring at the walls of a nursing home.

And so Mrs. Cahn was not exercised by the speed of the careening van. The others were, however. Finally, one of the scholars protested to the interpreter who relayed the protest to the driver who laughed, raising his arms high.

"He says," relayed the interpreter, "that we are in the hands of God."

Mrs. Cahn laughed, too, and then rested her head back for a little nap.

She was awakened by the babble of the group, for now they had reached level ground—they had been too terrified to speak before. Mrs. Cahn looked out her window. They were on the floor of a valley, what she had seen from above, that spacious, green and empty peace. The barren mountain slopes flowed down to it in long, pastel colored chutes, pale blue, pink, lavender, though in the protected places where snow had lain and long soaked the earth, a green as vivid as the spring wheat of the valley floor. There appeared to be nothing in the valley except for a stone aqueduct passing far out into the fields from a grove of willows, its sides overflowing with sheets of water, silvered by the sun. The beauty and stillness of the place almost brought tears to Mrs. Cahn's fine eyes and so to distract herself, she moved across the aisle to see what lay on the other side.

It was a teahouse, a long, one-story, whitewashed building with a thatch roof which overhung the front of the building to form a covered veranda. On this veranda, against the teahouse wall, stood a long bench painted pink. Pink! Of all colors to paint a bench, the oddity of it delighting Mrs. Cahn. And, of course, the customers might sit there, splattered with the sunlight filtering through the thatch, drinking tea, gazing out at the stillness and beauty of their valley.

As soon as the interpreter announced that this was not their destination, their valley lay another hour ahead, and that they had stopped only that the driver might buy a Pepsi Cola, Mrs. Cahn decided, yes, she would get off and sit on that pink bench and gaze out at her valley, at her peace. They could pick her up on the van's return.

There was much protest. The scholars insisted that they could not be responsible. Someone suggested that if she was determined on this questionable course, she must at least leave her purse on the van, for otherwise it might be taken from her. The interpreter, a city boy who had frequented few country teahouses, consulted the driver. The driver raised his arms high. The old woman looked like a queen, he said. The people at the teahouse would think so too and show her deference. The interpreter translated. The scholars and the rest reluctantly agreed but privately they had their opinions of this strange old woman.

"I shall alight," Mrs. Cahn announced. "Alight" not "get off" and indeed "alight" better described her stately descent from the van into the dust of the teahouse yard. When the van revved its motor to depart, she turned around. They were at the window of the van, staring at her, waving, but looking puzzled and hurt, as if she had somehow let them down. She waved back to them, dismissively, and then walked over to the pink bench and sat down.

So she sat there, gazing at her valley, not thinking, only existing. She even, unconsciously, let her shoulders slump a little. Not for long. A dark middle-aged man in pajamas and with a three-day stubble came out the teahouse door bearing a tray. There was a tiny bowl of what looked like rock candy on it and a small glass of tea in a dented silver holder. With a slight nod and a slight bow, and on his face a scowl, or perhaps a look of puzzlement, she wasn't sure, he offered her the tray with both hands.

"*Merci*," she said, taking the tray with both hands. On arriving in foreign places, Mrs. Cahn always learned the word or phrase for "thank you." It worked as well here as anywhere, for after a short pause the man smiled at her and then began speaking Persian. She shook her head. He laughed and nodded. For a few moments he continued to gaze at her, the smile, however, soon replaced by the look of puzzlement, though now it was friendlier. Finally, his hand across his heart, he walked backward, away from her. At the teahouse door he whispered to a little boy, the child nodding, then running off.

Now Mrs. Cahn noticed that a group of children, women, and a man or two were facing her across the teahouse yard, drifting in, it occurred to her, much as the chorus does in an opera, at first unnoticed. On their faces there was the same staring puzzlement she had seen on the teahouse keeper's face. She waved and smiled at them. They smiled back, but briefly, replaced by the staring puzzlement. She tried to ignore them, looking out at her valley, but there they stood in the foreground, distracting her. There was nothing she could do about them, staring at her as though she was a freak. She wanted to stand up and say "shoo" to them. Then, laughing to herself, she realized that to them, of course, she was a freak.

This went on for a time until she noticed a moving cloud of dust on the road below. Near the teahouse a man on a horse rode out of the dust, a young man she sensed, something odd on his head. When he reached the onlookers, he slid off the horse with a speed and agility which confirmed to her that he was young, still in his teens, she surmised. Throwing the reins to a boy, he walked toward her. She was intrigued by his hat. It appeared to be made of tan felt with wings or upstanding flaps to either side. Then she looked down at his face and caught her breath, for he was very beautiful.

As long as Mrs. Cahn could remember she had thrilled to male beauty. Even now, an old woman, she could still be taken by it; the nutbrown skin, small, beautifully formed ears, the exquisite line of nose and lips, and the eyes, like hers, enormous, black and shining.

"Madame," he called to her.

"Yes," she answered, rather flustered.

"Welcome to us. But what are you doing here?" he added sternly.

"I am resting," she replied, "and enjoying the view."

Frowning, he turned to face the valley, his hand raised to shade his eyes, scanning it as though there were something he had failed to see. He turned back, shaking his head. "How did you come to us?" She explained. He stared at her, looking both incredulous and suspicious. Suddenly he said, "Excuse," and after a little bow, he went into the teahouse. To check her story with the teahouse keeper, she surmised.

When he came out, she patted the place next to her on the bench. "Do sit down and talk to me."

He smiled, for the first time, but shook his head, and then

he placed his hand across his heart and said, "I am Habib, your servant."

"I am delighted to meet you, Habib." More like captivated, she thought to herself. And now especially that he was smiling. She felt weak, the old sign of infatuation. Looking away from him to compose herself, she said, "And if I may ask, how is it that you speak English so well?"

"It is the kindness of you," he said. "You see we are a tribe here," his arm sweeping out in a grand arc, "and I am the teacher. I go with us when we move to the mountains in summer—for our sheep, you know—and to the hot country below in winter and I have a tent, special, and the children come to me. The English," he shrugged, "the tutor to the children of our Khan, he knows it and he learned me some."

"I would say more than some," she said, and then hearing laughter, she looked beyond him. The opera chorus had drawn closer and they were smiling too. Now, better able to see them, she liked them; they looked healthy and their smiles were truthful as though they were truly pleased to see her. And their clothes! Like gypsy women, she thought, such a gush of color and the gold ornaments, bracelets, lots of them, and strings of gold coins strung across some kind of headdress. She noticed also that when those who were laughing saw her looking at them, they put a hand before their face. An old gentility, if she remembered rightly. Had not her grandmother said it was rude to laugh before one's elders? And that reminded her of her own lapse. "Habib, forgive me. I neglected to introduce myself. I am Mrs. Cahn, from America."

He stared at her. Then shook his head, scowling. "Khan! Khan, you say?"

"Yes, Cahn," she replied.

"You are the wife of a khan?"

"Yes," she paused. Something was not quite right. "Yes," she went on, "but he died several years ago."

"*Khodah biamorzeh*. I don't know how to say in English… that God may care for him. And was he a great khan, his tribe strong and courageous?"

Now she finally understood. Khan and Cahn. They sounded much the same, only his more guttural than hers. "Ah yes," she said, "he was a great khan indeed." How it would have pleased him to be called a khan. Indeed he was always telling people what to do but protecting them as well, caring for them. Dear Marty. She had loved him so much. But was his tribe courageous? She thought of her in-laws. "I'm not sure about courageous, Habib, but I think it can be said that they were very fierce, very fierce indeed." She laughed.

"But you are not red," Habib said.

"Red!" Mrs. Cahn exclaimed.

"Yes, are not the American tribes red?"

"Oh, I see. You mean the Indians. No, I am not of that tribe. And the Indians are not red, Habib. That is a myth."

"What is myth?"

"Something which claims to be true and isn't. There are a lot of myths around."

A man from the chorus called out to Habib. Habib replied with much sternness, almost severity. More and more it seemed to Mrs. Cahn that his beauty was an overlay, that beneath the boy there was a man, or soon would be, power, force, and she was reminded of one of her favorite artifacts at the museum and its exquisite chasing…on a blade of steel. But what was this word *bibi* that he repeated several times when pointing to her and which the chorus echoed when looking at her? "What is *bibi*?" she asked when he turned back to her.

"It's what we call the wife of a khan. So you are *Bibi* Madame."

He frowned. "No, *Bibi Khanum*, the sound is better. *Khanum* is what we call for Madame."

Bibi Khanum. It quite pleased Mrs. Cahn and she smiled as warmly as she could at him and affected a little shiver of delight, this beautiful boy bestowing a title on her. She had always wanted a title, thought she deserved one. To be a duchess, for example. *Bibi* was not quite in the same league but not bad, a tribal queen. She leaned back, even more erect than usual, against the teahouse wall.

Habib moved a little toward her. "*Bibi Khanum*, have you no hunger?"

She didn't quite take in what he said, absorbed as she was in watching his movement, the grace of it, the flow of his body putting her in mind of some of the great dancers she had seen. How, she wondered, had he come by it? Though she saw it, too, in the chorus of onlookers, the ease of their bodies and of their movement, an ease which somehow eased her too, stilled her, as gazing at the valley stilled her. That was the magic of the place, from the moment she had looked down into its green peace from the mountain road. And now the people, too, the valley before her, the sun-dappled teahouse wall warm against her back. She felt so light, all heaviness swept out of her, as if she were young again.

"But have you no hunger?" Habib repeated.

"No, I have no hunger but what is this?" and she pointed to a little girl who had left the ranks of the onlookers and now stood a short distance from her, the child's head down but eyes up, gazing at her. Mrs. Cahn patted her knee. "How do you say 'come,' Habib?"

"*Beyah*," he said, walking over to the child, placing one hand behind her back, grasping her fingers with the other, leading her to Mrs. Cahn. In shyness the child looked at the ground but at the same time held out her hand, the clenched fingers slowly opening. In the nest of the tiny palm lay a large, blue bead. "Oh," crowed Habib, "a gift, a gift, yes, to remind you of how our sky is blue, so blue."

Mrs. Cahn took the bead and raised it to her lips, putting her other hand on the child's head. The child moved out from under her hand but now looked forthrightly at her, smiling. "Oh Habib. Tell her my thanks, that I shall always keep it, always. What can I...?" Then she remembered; a tiny, enameled bird with a pin on the back of it that she had bought the night before in a tourist shop for one of her granddaughters. She took it from her purse and, after showing it to the child, pinned it on her blouse.

For the first time the child spoke. It was like a little declaration, or so it sounded to Mrs. Cahn, so formal and with a kind of cadence to it. "What does she say, Habib?"

"She says *dast-e shomah dard nakoneh*."

"Yes, but in English?"

"It says," he paused, "it says 'may your hand not feel pain.' We say it when someone gives us something, to give honor to them."

Mrs. Cahn stared at him and then at the child. "Oh! How beautiful," she finally, softly said. Then she leaned her head against the teahouse wall and closed her eyes. She wanted— even though she knew it was a rudeness—to be still for a little while, to let her mind wander among the visions of the day: the valley and its pastel mountains sloping down to the spring wheat, the pink bench against the teahouse wall, Habib appearing from the cloud of dust, the chorus hung with gold, that bit of sky in the cup of the child's hand, her own old hand...without pain. She would have been content to have kept thinking of these things, lulled by them, but she sensed that someone had approached. It was Habib with a tray of tea, a glass for himself, hers in the dented silver holder.

"Repeat it, Habib."

"Repeat what?"

"*Dast*...whatever it is...the pain. I want to remember it. Three times and I shall say it after you and then I shall have it; I'm very good at languages."

"Now that is that," she said after repeating the phrase and the English as well. "Now I have it. And now Habib come sit over here on the bench with me." He obeyed but chose a spot a yard or so down the bench from her. It irked her. She wanted him close to her so that she might smell him. She knew it was an idiotic notion, the notion that such beauty must have a fragrance but still...and she scooted down the bench to sit beside him. There was in fact a fragrance but was it simply the fragrance of the place itself, that occasional whiff of sweetness she had noticed in the air.

"Now tell me, Habib," she began, "about here. Where am I?"

"You are in a famous place, *Bibi Khanum*! Our *il*, our tribe, love it much. We stop on our way down from the mountains, always."

"Famous! Really?" How could it be famous, she wondered. It was empty.

"The lion." He stood up.

"Lion!"

"Yes, but all are gone now. Shot." He shook his head. "It was a bad thing to do." He turned and pointed to the valley. "It was where they played, the lion, until they were all shot, long ago." He shook his head. "And then famous number two."

"Number two? Oh, yes, I see."

"Famous number two is *narges*."

"I don't understand."

"I don't know in English. White with gold eye."

146

She shook her head.

"It has such a good smell, *narges*." He brought his fingers to his nose.

Then it came to her. The fragrance in the air and white with a golden center. Narcissus, of course. "But where?"

He pointed to the valley. "Everywhere."

"But who planted them?"

"I don't understand."

"Who put them there?"

He frowned. "God put them."

"Ah, yes, I see." Wild narcissi, she supposed.

"And now the large famous, *Bibi Khanum*," Habib went on, "*Hazrat-e Ali*."

"What is that?"

"Our Imam. Our great Imam. He is next to God."

"I see," said Mrs. Cahn, affecting gravity.

"He was here!"

"No!"

"Yes!" Habib pointed to the ground. "Yes, here, but he wanted sleep and so went there under a tree," he gestured to the willow grove, "and then do you know…"

"What?" Mrs. Cahn felt quite caught up in the story.

"Ali awakened and what do you think he saw before him? The lion!"

"Oh no, no." Mrs. Cahn was tired of hearing of misfortunes, calamities, tragedy. She had no real idea of who Ali was nor did she care but nonetheless she did not want him eaten by a lion.

"No, no worry," Habib said, seeing the consternation on her face. "You see his mouth was full of *narges* and he dropped them at Ali's feet."

"Oh Habib, Habib," Mrs. Cahn said, raising her arms above her head and softly clapping. "What a wonderful, wonderful story."

"Is not a story," Habib said and in his excitement he sat down next to her. "Is true, is true *Bibi Khanum*. We know."

"Yes, yes, of course," Mrs. Cahn said and to reassure him she lightly touched his wrist.

Mrs. Cahn had not had an unhappy life but it had not been especially happy either. On the other hand, there had been, at least until recent years, many of what she believed the French called *le petit bonheur*, the little happinesses. This was one of them, now, here, intensely so. "I'm so grateful," she said, almost touching Habib's wrist again.

"I don't understand," he said.

Raising her arm, she made a circling gesture with her hand. "These past few hours, so grateful I am, for everything."

And it was then she heard the van's bleating horn and saw it below arriving in a cloud of dust. "They have come," she said. "Ah, they have come, Habib, the people I came with. To take me back." She stood up, reluctant to leave the warmth of the tea-house wall, reluctant to leave everything, the valley, the silver-sheeted aqueduct, the chorus still there, smiling, the teahouse, her bench, the strong and beautiful Habib, wishing so that she could stay but knowing that it was, of course, impossible, knowing, too, that the perfection would not have lasted, it never had, never would. At least there has been this.

She took a step forward but stiff from sitting for so long, she faltered. When Habib stepped quickly to her side, she put her arm through his and then slowly they began to walk together down the slope toward the van, the chorus in a straggle behind them. It amused Mrs. Cahn to think how she and Habib must look to the astonished—and, she hoped, disapproving—tour group: her long, gray skirts sweeping the dust, the wide-brimmed straw hat bobbing up and down on her nodding head, Habib in his black, bell-bottomed tribal trousers and a vest as patterned and colorful as some old tapestry, the curious hat with its flaps, its little ears—the old woman, the beautiful boy, and the straggle of their court.

At the steps to the van Habib put his hand under Mrs. Cahn's elbow. Reaching the first step, she grasped the hand rail and then turned around to wish them all goodbye. Before she could begin, Habib, stepping back from the van, raised his hand.

"*Bibi Khanum*, you have honored us. You are a great *Bibi*. I see it in you, hear it from you. May you go with God."

"But Habib…" she began. Before she could continue one of the women from the chorus had appeared before her with a sheaf of narcissus.

Rarely in her life had Mrs. Cahn been overwhelmed, overcome, at a loss. She was almost always ready. But this time…and then she remembered. Taking the narcissus in her arms, she slowly said: "*Dast-e shomah dard nakoneh*, may your hands not feel pain for all that you have given me."

To calls of *Bibi Khanum, Bibi Khanum*, she turned to pull herself up the second step but stopped, turned back, and though she knew she shouldn't, she blew Habib a kiss. Then she turned back again and ascended the final step.

The van reached Shiraz an hour later. Except for Mrs. Cahn, one of the scholars was the last to leave. "Upsy-daisy, Miriam," he called to her, "we're back, upsy-daisy," and then he ducked out the door. The driver climbed back into the van to retrieve his Pepsi Cola bottle from the floorboard. Seeing Mrs. Cahn, he called to her. "*Bibi Khanum*." Then he walked down the aisle to her seat at the rear. She sat, erect as always, staring down at the narcissus cradled in her lap. "*Bibi Khanum*," he called again, this time frowning and lightly touching her. And then he knew. And again he called her name but now so softly, so very gently. For Mrs. Cahn was dead.

ABOUT THE AUTHOR

Terence O'Donnell lived in Iran from 1957–71 before returning to his native Oregon, where he wrote *Garden of the Brave in War: Recollections of Iran* (Univ. of Chicago Press), a memoir praised by critics as "a gem" and "a literary classic." He now divides his time between an apartment in Portland and a cottage on the Washington coast.